CLASSIC

STAR WARS®

THE REBEL STORM

writer
Archie Goodwin

artist
Al Williamson

art assist
Allen Nunis
(parts 10-14)
Monty Sheldon
(part 12)

colorists
Steve Buccellato
(parts 8-11, 13, 14)
Ray Murtaugh
(part 12)

introduction
Kevin J. Anderson

series editors
Bob Cooper
Anina Bennett

collection editor
Lynn Adair

collection designers
Brian Gogolin
& Scott Tice

CLASSIC STAR WARS®

THE REBEL STORM

By
Archie Goodwin
&
Al Williamson

DARK HORSE COMICS®

MIKE RICHARDSON
publisher
NEIL HANKERSON
executive vp
DAVID SCROGGY
vp of publishing
LOU BANK
vp of sales & marketing
ANDY KARABATSOS
vp of finance
MARK ANDERSON
general counsel
DIANA SCHUTZ
editor in chief
RANDY STRADLEY
creative director
CINDY MARKS
director of production & design
MARK COX
art director
SEAN TIERNEY
computer graphics director
CHRIS CREVISTON
director of accounting
MICHAEL MARTENS
marketing director
TOD BORLESKE
sales & licensing director
MARK ELLINGTON
director of operations
DALE LAFOUNTAIN
director of m.i.s.

CLASSIC STAR WARS® VOLUME TWO

This book is based on the classic Star Wars® newspaper strip and collects
issues 8-14 of the Dark Horse comic-book series *Classic Star Wars*.

Published by
Dark Horse Comics, Inc.
10956 SE Main Street
Milwaukie, OR 97222

ISBN: 1-56971-106-2
First edition: July 1995

10 9 8 7 6 5 4 3 2

Printed in Canada

INTRODUCTION

by Kevin J. Anderson

When these guys say "Classic," they mean exactly that.

The Goodwin and Williamson *Classic Star Wars* comics — which you now hold in your sweaty hands (but don't grip too tightly, because you'll ruin the collectability) — were written at the time of the films, from 1981 to 1984. These stories fill in the three years between *A New Hope* and *The Empire Strikes Back.*

And a lot of adventures can happen in three years.

The precursors to these comics were originally done as newspaper strips by the famed writer/ artist team of Archie Goodwin and Al Williamson. In re-printing these stories, though, Dark Horse Comics has not taken the quick and dirty route of slapping old newspaper panels on a page and repub-lishing it in comic-book format.

Sketch by Al Williamson

What you see here is a completely different work of art, modified and reshaped to fit *this* form. The art has been re-inked, touched up in some cases, re-drawn in others, colored, and rearranged, sometimes even rewritten to eliminate the repetition that was required for its newspaper-serial incarnation.

However, the pacing of these stories is still reminiscent of the original form. No time for a relaxed sigh or deep introspection — go read Proust if that's what you're looking for — these *Classic Star Wars* comics are a thrill a minute, artistically dazzling stuff every step of the way — mind-boggling ideas and visuals to sweep you along.

Read this collection with your seat belt on.

For numerically challenged readers, I should point out that this is *volume two* of the *Classic Star Wars* collections. Briefly, for those of you who don't have volume one — *go out and buy it.* That'll be much more interesting than a quick plot summary anyway.

One of the best parts of volume one is a fascinating introduction by Archie Goodwin about the daunting restrictions and expectations of working on a dramatic newspaper strip: the need for major action every two or three panels, the stuttering re-dundancy from day to day, and the need to cater to readers who never miss an installment as well as those who read only the Sunday paper or those who skip Saturdays.

That's why you don't see any full-page splashes or two-page spreads here — bear in mind that these were designed to run in a narrow format in a newspaper, right next to "Peanuts" or the "Wizard of Id." But Al Williamson manages to transcend the format by selecting his perspectives, rescuing "talking heads" scenes by taking us to a distant or alien viewpoint, and showing exotic landscapes, refreshingly weird aliens, and bizarre contraptions — in short, all the ingredients that made *Star Wars* so popular.

The first Goodwin and Williamson collection took us to Imperial starship construction yards, then to a planet of scavengers riding murderous flying serpents, a drifting graveyard in space surrounding a collapsing star — and finally to the underwater base on the ocean world of Aquaris, where we met the (possibly) treacherous but definitely beautiful Silver Fyre, a notorious space pirate from Han's smuggling days, who now claims to have sided with the Rebels . . . but she may have other plans in the works.

Since the major resurgence in *Star Wars* interest with the release of Timothy Zahn's *Heir to the Empire* from Bantam and Tom Veitch and Cam Kennedy's *Dark Empire* series from Dark Horse, a wealth of new adventures has been available to readers.

All of us writers have been busily trying to fill in the holes and gaps of *Star Wars* history, building stories about every offhand comment in the films. I know, because I did it myself with the Spice Mines of Kessel and the Kessel Run in my novel *Jedi Search*; Tim Zahn did it with the Bothans in his trilogy; and others have worked on Lando Calrissian's Battle of Tanaab. My own anthologies *Tales From The Mos Eisley Cantina* (July 1995), *Tales from Jabba's Palace*, and *Bounty Hunters* (both forthcoming) give the background stories on all the characters we met in those respective scenes. *Star Wars* just gets bigger and bigger.

But Williamson and Goodwin were filling in the blanks long before any of this. In the first volume of *Classic Star Wars*, we saw Han Solo's run-in with the bounty hunter on Ord Mantell, which Han cites as his reason for needing to leave Echo Base on Hoth in *The Empire Strikes Back*, and we witness the construction of Darth Vader's enormous flagship, the Super Star Destroyer *Executor*.

In this second collection, we learn more about the mysterious Massassi temple ruins on Yavin Four. We see how the Rebels meet up with Admiral Ackbar and the Calamarians, how they plan their escape from their secret base on the jungle moon, and how they choose the frozen world of Hoth as their next hide-out.

But these aren't just filler details. In this collection, we also see the end of the treacherous adventures on the water world of Aquaris. A horrific, near-indestructible night beast emerges from the abandoned temple ruins of the Rebel Base on Yavin Four carrying a devastating secret from the past. Han Solo and Chewbacca find themselves fighting in gladiatorial combat to gain possession of a power gem that may help them destroy Vader's battleship *Executor*.

Luke Skywalker encounters a man who claims to be Obi-Wan Kenobi, and — together with a band of desert nomads — they destroy an Imperial installation . . . or is it all just part of a plot from Darth Vader? The *Millennium Falcon* is trapped by enormous mud worms and dragged to the bottom of a swamp while Han and Luke try to avoid capture from Imperial patrols. And General Dodonna's son barely survives a devastating Imperial space attack. Is he a hero, or a coward, or a traitor?

Readers of the *Star Wars: Dark Lords of the Sith* comics (written by Tom Veitch and me) and its sequel *The Sith War* will learn much more about the origin of the Massassi temples on Yavin Four as well as the night beast and its true mission. Nothing is as simple as it seems because the *Star Wars* universe is vast and complex, with a huge collection of interconnected stories that we have only begun to tap.

I am currently at work writing *The Star Wars Chronology*, a Michener-style tome that tells the whole saga of more than five thousand years of *Star Wars* history *in novel form* — in other words, you can read it rather than just flip through it like an encyclopedia. The *Chronology* will begin five millennia before *A New Hope*, during the Golden Age of the Sith, and will end 25 years later, with Han and Leia's children becoming full Jedi Knights. My resources include all the Dark Horse comics, the Lando Calrissian and Han Solo adventures from Del Rey books, the three films, the *Classic Star Wars* strips, the numerous sequel novels from Bantam, and the new Young Jedi Knights series from Berkley Boulevard.

The Star Wars Chronology is scheduled to be published immediately before the release of the next *Star Wars* films, and readers will at last be able to see that all of these disparate pieces really *do* fit together. Honest! Trust me — and keep reading.

—Kevin J. Anderson
July 1995

PART 8

Unable to talk his way out of the hunting party... Han finds himself partnered with *SILVER FYRE*.

LUKE'S RIDING WITH HER SECOND-IN-COMMAND, KRAAKEN...

...AND CHEWIE WITH *ANOTHER* OF SILVER'S PIRATES! I'VE SET THE DROIDS UP AS *BAIT*, BUT NOW THEY'RE *UNPROTECTED* WHILE WE'RE STUCK IN THESE *AQUA-SKIMMERS!*

WHAT ARE YOU *PULLING*, SILVER? WHY DID YOU *SEPARATE* LUKE, CHEWIE, AN' ME FOR THIS HUNTING PARTY?

ACTUALLY, IT WAS *KRAAKEN'S* IDEA.

MY SECOND-IN-COMMAND DID SOME *EAVESDROPPING* YESTERDAY. DESPITE PRINCESS LEIA'S ASSURANCES, YOU OBVIOUSLY WON'T FORGET MY PAST AND ACCEPT ME AS AN *ALLY*.

I'D SOONER ACCEPT A *USED BANTHA* AS PAYMENT FROM *JABBA THE HUTT!*

SUPPOSE I SAVE THE *LIFE* OF ONE OF YOUR *FRIENDS?*

AQUARIS HAS PLENTY OF UNDERWATER CREATURES THAT SOMETIMES THREATEN OUR *BASE*, HAN--

AND YOU WERE GONNA *LET* ONE ATTACK LUKE'S OR CHEWIE'S AQUA-SKIMMER...

...SO YOU COULD *RESCUE* THEM AND CHANGE MY *MIND* ABOUT YOU?

THAT WAS *KRAAKEN'S* PLAN. I DECIDED TO ADD A SLIGHT *VARIATION*...

...IT'S CALLED *LEVELING* WITH YOU. I'LL CONTACT KRAAKEN TO *ABANDON* THE SCHEME BEFORE THERE'S TROUBLE.

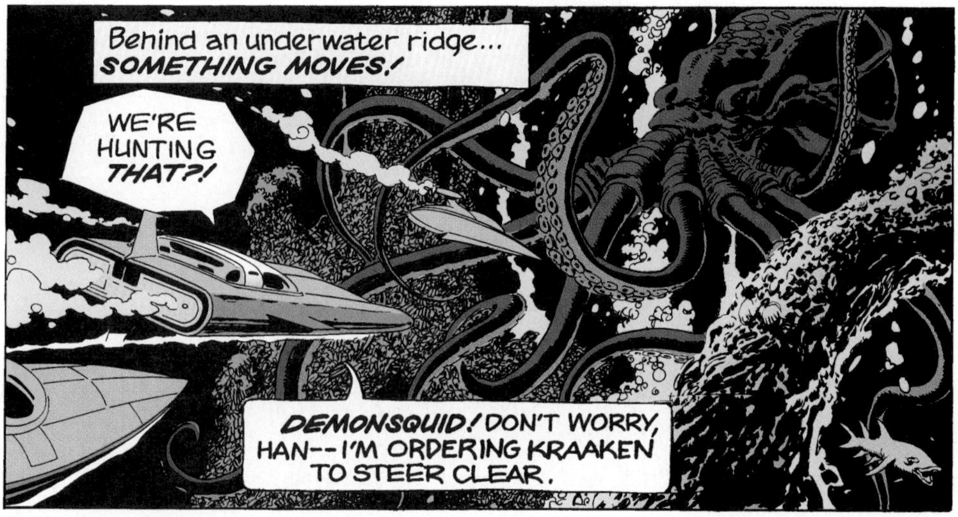
Behind an underwater ridge... SOMETHING MOVES!
WE'RE HUNTING THAT?!
DEMONSQUID! DON'T WORRY, HAN--I'M ORDERING KRAAKEN TO STEER CLEAR.

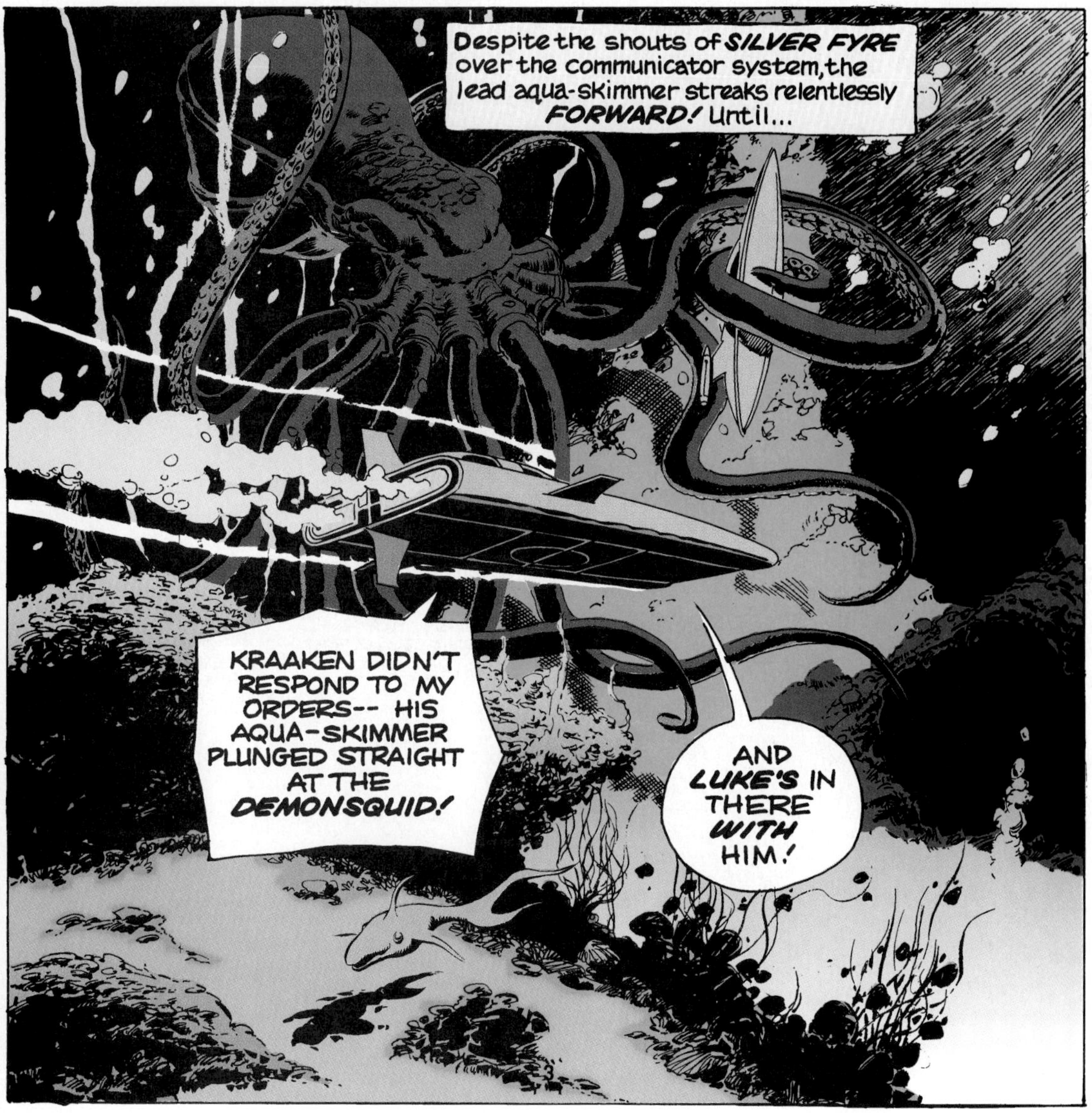
Despite the shouts of SILVER FYRE over the communicator system, the lead aqua-skimmer streaks relentlessly FORWARD! Until...
KRAAKEN DIDN'T RESPOND TO MY ORDERS-- HIS AQUA-SKIMMER PLUNGED STRAIGHT AT THE DEMONSQUID!
AND LUKE'S IN THERE WITH HIM!

YOU AND KRAAKEN WERE SETTING UP A *PHONY RESCUE*-- CAN YOU DO IT FOR *REAL?!*

I CONFESSED TO THAT TO PROVE I'VE *CHANGED...*

BUT BECOMING RESPECTABLE ENOUGH TO JOIN THE REBEL ALLIANCE HASN'T MADE ME ABANDON *ALL* THE SKILLS I DEVELOPED AS A SPACE PIRATE.'

The ray blast shocks the giant mollusk into dropping its *PREY!* But...

THEIR SKIMMER'S *SHATTERING,* SILVER! THEY'LL *DROWN--* IF THAT *THING* DOESN'T GRAB 'EM AGAIN.'

THERE'S *SURVIVAL GEAR* UNDER YOUR SEAT, HAN.'

Donning it, the Corellian space captain swiftly exits through the tiny undersea craft's emergency escape hatch...

HELP'S *COMIN',* KID-- IF THE OTHERS KEEP THAT *MONSTER* OCCUPIED!

Led by Silver Fyre, the remaining aqua-skimmers fight to drive off the demonsquid...

...as Han reaches the wreck!

LUKE!

Breaking Luke from the wreckage, Han is clamping a spare survival mask on his unconscious friend...

...when DISASTER strikes!

Silver Fyre's voice echoes in alarm over the aqua-skimmers' comlink...

THE DEMONSQUID HAS SOLO! STOP SHOOTING--WE MIGHT HIT HIM!

But if the *MILLENNIUM FALCON'S* captain risks abandoning his aqua-skimmer for an emergency rescue...

...can his *FIRST MATE* be far behind?

And having armed himself with a jagged shard from the wreckage of Luke's craft, *THE WOOKIEE STRIKES!*

The demonsquid's tentacle spasms in *PAIN* from Chewbacca's attack...

...allowing Han to slip *FREE* with Luke!

COMMANDER FYRE! THE WOOKIEE FREED SOLO AND SKYWALKER FROM THE *DEMONSQUID,* B-BUT--

IT'S FORGOTTEN *US* AND GONE FOR *THEM!*

AND THERE'S NO WAY TO CALL WHO'S GOING TO OVERTAKE WHO *FIRST!*

As Silver Fyre moves up behind the relentless monster...

...for the first time her skimmer guns have a *CLEAR SHOT* at the creature's vital brain sac!

The battle ends...

...and the demonsquid sinks into Aquaris' endless ocean depths.

But as the rescued trio is picked up...

KRAAKEN WASN'T *IN* THAT WRECK WITH LUKE?!

THEIR SKIMMER WAS ON *AUTO-PILOT*...

...AND THE KID WAS *STUN-BLASTED* BEFORE THE HUNT STARTED.

I WAS *WRONG* ABOUT YOU BEING A TRAITOR. IT'S YOUR *SECOND-IN-COMMAND!*

The aqua-skimmers race back toward the Freeholder's underwater base...

RADIO AHEAD, SILVER! KRAAKEN SUCKERED US *ALL* OUT HERE...

...TO GIVE HIM A CLEAR SHOT AT GETTING THE *SECRET INFO* LUKE'S DROIDS ARE CARRYING! BUT MAYBE--

HAN...

"...THERE'S *NO RESPONSE* FROM OUR COMMUNICATIONS CENTER!"

SILVER, CAN'T YOU PUSH THIS TIN FISH ANY *FASTER?*

IT'S NOT THE *MILLENNIUM FALCON*-- WE DON'T HAVE *HYPERDRIVE!*

THE BASE ISN'T *FAR,* THOUGH. HOW'S *LUKE?*

HE'LL BE *FINE* WHEN THE STUN BLAST WEARS OFF. UNTIL HE LEARNS...

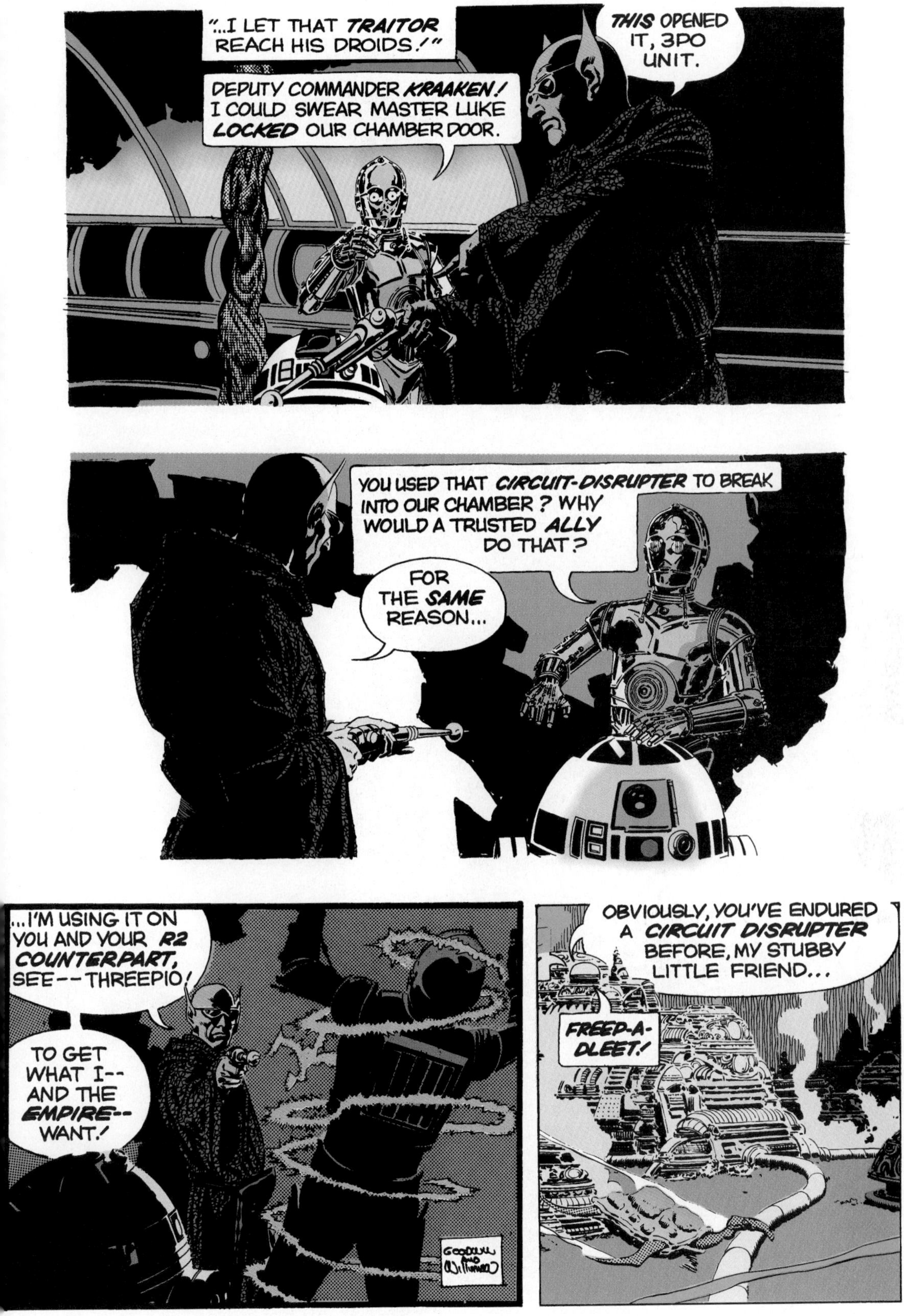

"...I LET THAT TRAITOR REACH HIS DROIDS!"
DEPUTY COMMANDER KRAAKEN! I COULD SWEAR MASTER LUKE LOCKED OUR CHAMBER DOOR.
THIS OPENED IT, 3PO UNIT.
YOU USED THAT CIRCUIT-DISRUPTER TO BREAK INTO OUR CHAMBER? WHY WOULD A TRUSTED ALLY DO THAT?
FOR THE SAME REASON...
...I'M USING IT ON YOU AND YOUR R2 COUNTERPART, SEE--THREEPIO!
TO GET WHAT I--AND THE EMPIRE--WANT!
OBVIOUSLY, YOU'VE ENDURED A CIRCUIT DISRUPTER BEFORE, MY STUBBY LITTLE FRIEND...
FREEP-A-DLEET!

...IT CAN'T *HURT* YOU! BUT IT WILL CERTAINLY *ERASE* ANY SAFEGUARDS THAT MIGHT KEEP ME FROM RETRIEVING THE *INFORMATION* YOU CARRY!

PERHAPS THE NEXT TIME HAN SOLO *BAITS* A TRAP, HE'LL PICK SOMETHING THE REBEL ALLIANCE CAN AFFORD TO *LOSE!*

YOU DID A BRILLIANT JOB OF GETTING EVERYBODY OUT OF YOUR *WAY,* DEPUTY COMMANDER...

...ALMOST!

PRINCESS LEIA! H-HOW--?

OH, I'VE BEEN *WAITING* FOR YOU, KRAAKEN...

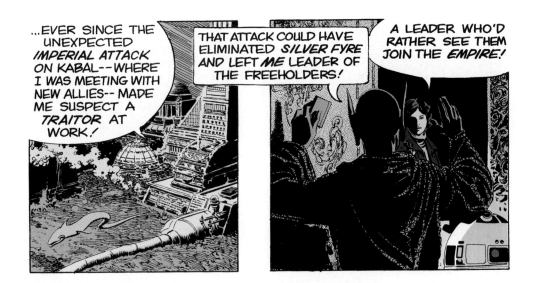

...EVER SINCE THE UNEXPECTED *IMPERIAL ATTACK* ON KABAL--WHERE I WAS MEETING WITH NEW ALLIES-- MADE ME SUSPECT A *TRAITOR* AT WORK!

THAT ATTACK COULD HAVE ELIMINATED *SILVER FYRE* AND LEFT *ME* LEADER OF THE FREEHOLDERS!

A LEADER WHO'D RATHER SEE THEM JOIN THE *EMPIRE!*

I COULDN'T BE CERTAIN THE TRAITOR I SUSPECTED WAS IN *YOUR* GROUP...

...BUT OUR DETOUR HERE WAS A PERFECT CHANCE TO *FIND OUT!*

AND I WAS SO BUSY TWISTING *HAN SOLO'S* CLUMSY ATTEMPT AT A *TRAP* TO MY ADVANTAGE--

YOU OVERLOOKED THE POSSIBILITY OF SOMEONE *ELSE* SETTING ONE!

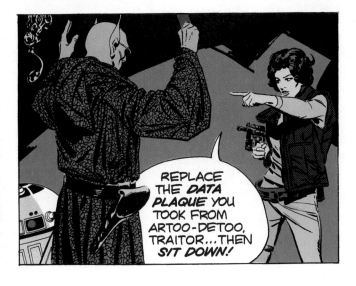

REPLACE THE *DATA PLAQUE* YOU TOOK FROM ARTOO-DETOO, TRAITOR...THEN *SIT DOWN!*

I'M HOLDING YOU HERE UNTIL HAN AND SILVER FYRE RETURN!

PRINCESS LEIA! DEPUTY COMMANDER KRAAKEN! WHAT'S GOING *ON?!*

THE REBELS HAVE TURNED *AGAINST* US, GUARD! THEY'RE SABOTAGING OUR BASE! *GET HER!*

For a moment the guard *HESITATES,* confused...

...which is *ALL* Kraaken needs!

Meanwhile, the aqua-skimmers return to the underwater base! But...

COMMANDER FYRE! THERE'S *SHOOTING* IN THE LIVING QUARTERS...

...A GUARD REPORTS *PRINCESS LEIA* SURPRISED DEPUTY COMMANDER *KRAAKEN* IN AN ACT OF *TREASON!*

GET HELP FOR *LUKE,* SILVER! I'VE GOT AN *IDEA...*

...IF IT'S NOT *TOO LATE!*

CAREFUL, YOUR HIGHNESS-- HE TOOK MY *BLASTER!*

YES, I *NOTICED!*

I HOPE YOU *ALSO* NOTICED I HAVE THE *DATA PLAQUE* FROM YOUR DROID, REBEL!

I'M *STILL* GETTING AWAY WITH THE *PRIZE!*

WHERE DOES THIS DOOR LEAD?

TO THE *LAUNCHING PLATFORM,* YOUR HIGHNESS-- HE'S *SURE* TO ESCAPE!

IT'S *SEALED!* KRAAKEN'S *MELTED* THE LOCKS FROM THE OTHER SIDE!

BY THE TIME WE GET HELP AND *BLAST* THROUGH, HE'LL BE *TAKING OFF!*

Somewhere above, the undersea base's launching platform begins to surface...

...carrying a *TRAITOR* in its personnel lift!

ATTENTION, HANGAR DROIDS-- THIS IS THE DEPUTY COMMANDER! HAVE OUR *FASTEST SHIP* WAITING FOR ME!

The *SURFACE!* Kraaken steps from the personnel lift...

...and finds an *OBSTACLE* between him and his escape craft!

KINDA *THOUGHT* YOU MIGHT HEAD THIS WAY, TRAITOR...SO I USED THE *AQUA-SKIMMER* TO GET HERE WHILE THE PLATFORM WAS STILL *RISING!*

GOOD THINKING, SOLO-- BUT IT WON'T HELP MUCH WHEN YOU'RE *DEAD!*

COULDN'T CHANCE *BLASTING* YOU, KRAAKEN-- MIGHT DESTROY THE *DATA* YOU'RE TRYING TO STEAL! BESIDES...

AFTER THE WAY YOU PLAYED SILVER FYRE AN' ME FOR *SUCKERS,* AN' ALMOST GOT *LUKE* KILLED...

...*THIS IS MORE SATISFYING!*

But as the traitor crashes to the launch platform's deck...

FOOL! YOU'VE GOT ME, BUT YOU'VE LOST THE PRECIOUS *DATA PLAQUE* FOREVER!

And the data plaque disappears into Aquaris's endless ocean.

KRAAKEN... YOU MISERABLE, TRAITOROUS *CREEP!*

EASY, HAN-- WATCH!

s the water where raaken threw the data aque violently erupts...

LEIA! WHAT--?

WHEN I TOOK OVER THE *TRAP* YOU SET UP, FLYBOY, I DID SOME *TAMPERING* WITH THE *BAIT!*

THAT THING WAS *BOOBY-TRAPPED?*

I COULDN'T VERY WELL USE THE *REAL INFORMATION* AS BAIT, NO ONE'S *THAT* RECKLESS...RIGHT?

UH... DEPENDS ON THE *CIRCUMSTANCES,* YOUR WORSHIP!

YOU COULD LET *OTHER PEOPLE* KNOW WHAT YOU'RE DOIN' SOMETIMES. SAVES... ER... *DUPLICATION* OF EFFORT!

RELAX, HAN. I *NEEDED* YOUR SCHEMING TO KEEP HIM FROM CATCHING ON TO *MINE!*

And... AT LEAST IN UNCOVERING *KRAAKEN'S* TREASON YOU'VE CLEARED THE *REST* OF US, PRINCESS.

NOW WE'LL CLEAR THE *EMPIRE*, SILVER-- *AWAY* FROM OUR YAVIN BASE!

As the *MILLENNIUM FALCON* departs Aquaris...

SILVER FYRE'S FREEHOLDERS ARE *JOINING* US, LEIA?

HAVING CAUGHT THE *TRAITOR* AMONG OUR NEW ALLIES...

"...IT'S SAFE TO USE THEIR *HELP* WITH THE SITUATION AT OUR *YAVIN BASE*, HAN."

A situation growing *WORSE!*

X-Wing fighters drive off some of the Imperial raiders...

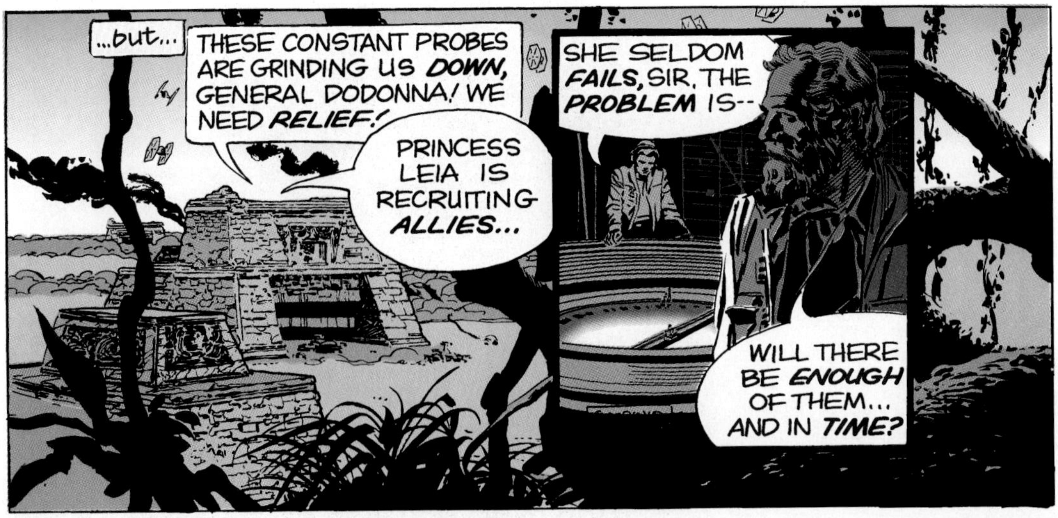
...but...
THESE CONSTANT PROBES ARE GRINDING US DOWN, GENERAL DODONNA! WE NEED RELIEF!
PRINCESS LEIA IS RECRUITING ALLIES...
SHE SELDOM FAILS, SIR. THE PROBLEM IS--
WILL THERE BE ENOUGH OF THEM... AND IN TIME?

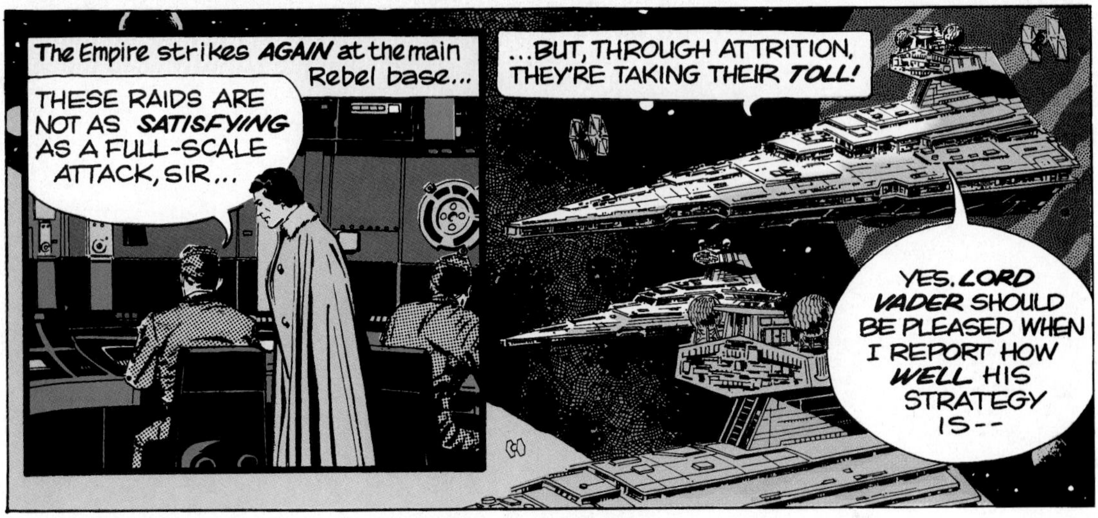
The Empire strikes AGAIN at the main Rebel base...
THESE RAIDS ARE NOT AS SATISFYING AS A FULL-SCALE ATTACK, SIR...
...BUT, THROUGH ATTRITION, THEY'RE TAKING THEIR TOLL!
YES. LORD VADER SHOULD BE PLEASED WHEN I REPORT HOW WELL HIS STRATEGY IS--

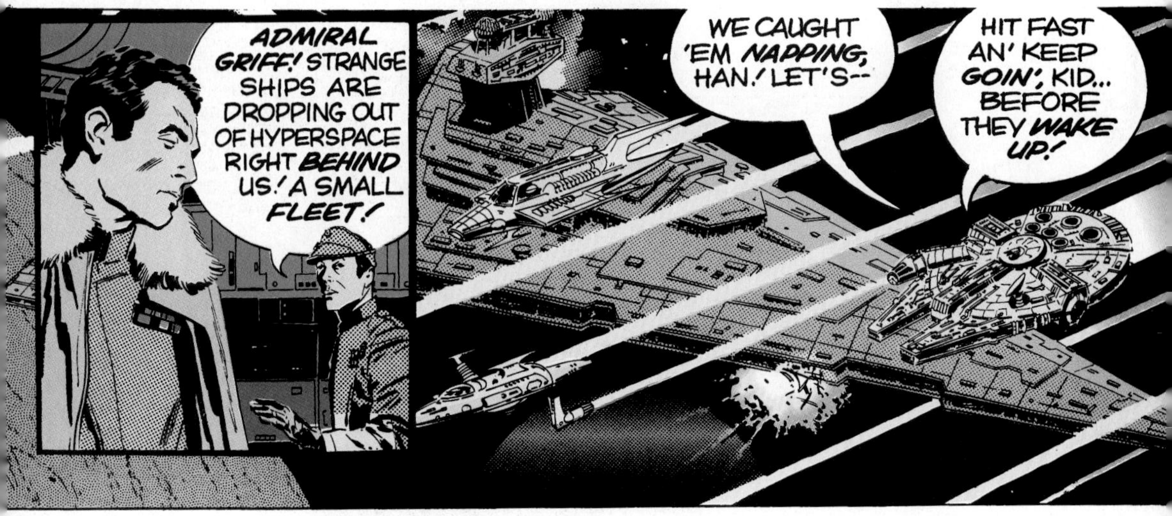
ADMIRAL GRIFF! STRANGE SHIPS ARE DROPPING OUT OF HYPERSPACE RIGHT BEHIND US! A SMALL FLEET!
WE CAUGHT 'EM NAPPING, HAN! LET'S--
HIT FAST AN' KEEP GOIN', KID... BEFORE THEY WAKE UP!

The *MILLENNIUM FALCON* zooms on to rout more enemies...

...unaware that an Imperial bomber plunges toward the surface...

...to *IMPACT* explosively in the Massassi ruins!

With the Imperial attack thwarted, the *MILLENNIUM FALCON* and its new allies touch down on Yavin's fourth moon...

LOOK, HAN! ONE OF THOSE EMPIRE JOBS WE KNOCKED DOWN CRASHED INTO PART OF THE RUINS!

YEAH, BUT IT'S A SECTION THE ALLIANCE DOESN'T USE NO BIG DEAL, LUKE!

But the explosive impact of the crash has reached far below the surface...

...disturbing *SOMETHING* long dormant!

Meanwhile... THEY'RE CELEBRATING OUR VICTORY OVER THE *IMPERIALS* TONIGHT, THREEPIO? GEE...WONDER IF *LEIA* HAS AN ESCORT?

And... BIG DOINGS PLANNED FOR THIS EVENING, CHEWIE! I'LL GIVE *HER WORSHIP* A BREAK AN' VOLUNTEER TO *TAKE* HER!

YAVIN BASE COMMAND SECTION. An unscheduled *MEETING* takes place...

HAN! I THOUGHT YOU WERE WORKING ON THE *FALCON!*

LUKE! UH...

...FIGURED YOU'D BE WITH THE *DROIDS*, KID! EXTRACTIN' ALL THAT *INFO* GATHERED ON YOUR SPY MISSION!

COULD THIS SOMEHOW INVOLVE *ME*...AND TONIGHT'S *CELEBRATION?*

LUKE, I'D *LOVE* TO GO TO THE VICTORY PARTY WITH YOU...

HEY! THE KID HASN'T OPENED HIS *MOUTH* YET, LEIA! BESIDES, I--

YOU'D *ALSO* BE A TOLERABLE CHOICE, HAN-- IF YOU *BEHAVED.* HOWEVER, *PROTOCOL* DICTATES THAT I ACCOMPANY *GENERAL DODONNA.* BESIDES...

...HE ASKED ME BEFORE *EITHER* OF YOU.!

As darkness approaches, ominous *SOUNDS* come from one section of the Massassi ruins...

ROWWWGH!

YOU SUDDENLY FEEL *UNEASY?* NO OFFENSE, CHEWIE, BUT HAVIN' A *WOOKIEE* AS MY DATE FOR THE BIG CELEBRATION DOESN'T THRILL *ME*, EITHER.!

But *OUTSIDE*, after the festivities begin...

WHAT'S GOING *ON* DOWN THERE ?! NO ONE'S SUPPOSED TO BE *NEAR* THIS TOWER UNLESS--

BASE CONTROL! *BASE CONTROL!* THIS IS OBSERVATION POST *THREE!*

Suddenly, there is the sound of *METAL* rending, as...

Within the ancient stone structures that house the Rebel Alliance...

YOU DON'T *MIND* HAVING AN OLD CODGER LIKE *ME* AS YOUR ESCORT, PRINCESS.?

ACTUALLY, IT SAVED ME FROM A RATHER *DIFFICULT* DECISION.

Suddenly... a thunderous *CRASH* shakes the hall.

W-WHAT--?!

IT CAME FROM *OUTSIDE!*

SOMETHING'S *TOPPLED* ONE OF THE OBSERVATION TOWERS... *IMPERIAL ATTACK!*

NO-- THE SKY'S *CLEAR!*

IT *MUST* BE THE *EMPIRE'S* WORK!

BLASTIN' THINGS TO *ATOMS* IS THEIR STYLE...

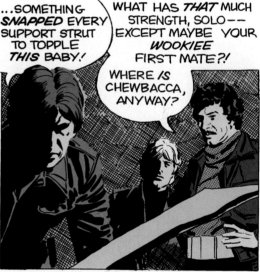

...SOMETHING *SNAPPED* EVERY SUPPORT STRUT TO TOPPLE *THIS* BABY!

WHAT HAS *THAT* MUCH STRENGTH, SOLO-- EXCEPT MAYBE YOUR *WOOKIEE* FIRST MATE?!

WHERE *IS* CHEWBACCA, ANYWAY?

I DON'T *LIKE* WHAT YOU'RE *HINTING,* FRIEND...!

EASY, HAN! EVERYONE'S *SHAKEN* OVER THE *WAY* THIS OBSERVATION TOWER *FELL...*

...NO ONE *SERIOUSLY* SUSPECTS *CHEWBACCA* OF BREAKING IT!

WELL, I SAW HIM *LEAVE* THE CELEBRATION JUST *BEFORE* THIS HAPPENED.

Chewbacca's search for what inspires his *UNEASINESS* has drawn him far from this evening's festivities.

But the sound of the observation tower's *COLLAPSE*...

...has brought the Wookiee running *BACK*...

...only to find his way suddenly *BLOCKED!*

Chewbacca has faced dangers of every variety throughout the galaxy, many *LARGER* than even *THIS* one.

Its sudden, ominous appearance inspires no *FEAR* in the *MILLENNIUM FALCON'S* first mate...

ROWWWRRK!

...which proves *UNFORTUNATE!*

HAN! THOSE *NOISES* FROM THE FOREST-- SOUNDS LIKE A *FIGHT!*

AND *LISTEN* TO THOSE GROWLS, LUKE! *CHEWIE'S* INVOLVED!

Involved...perhaps *FATALLY!*

PART 9

CHEWIE!

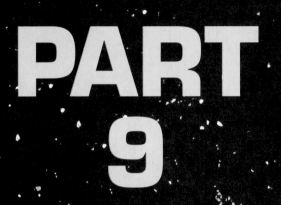

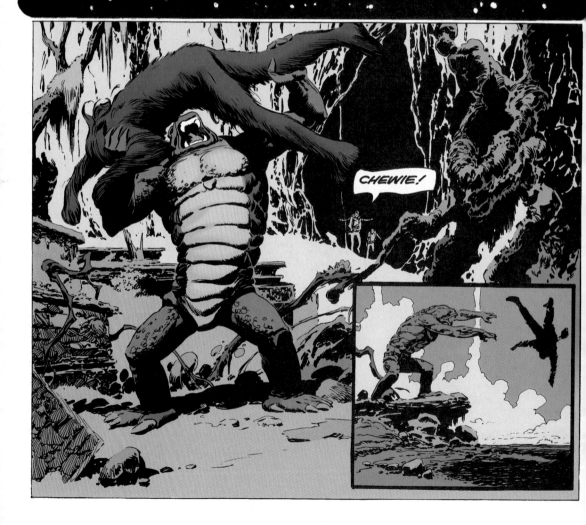

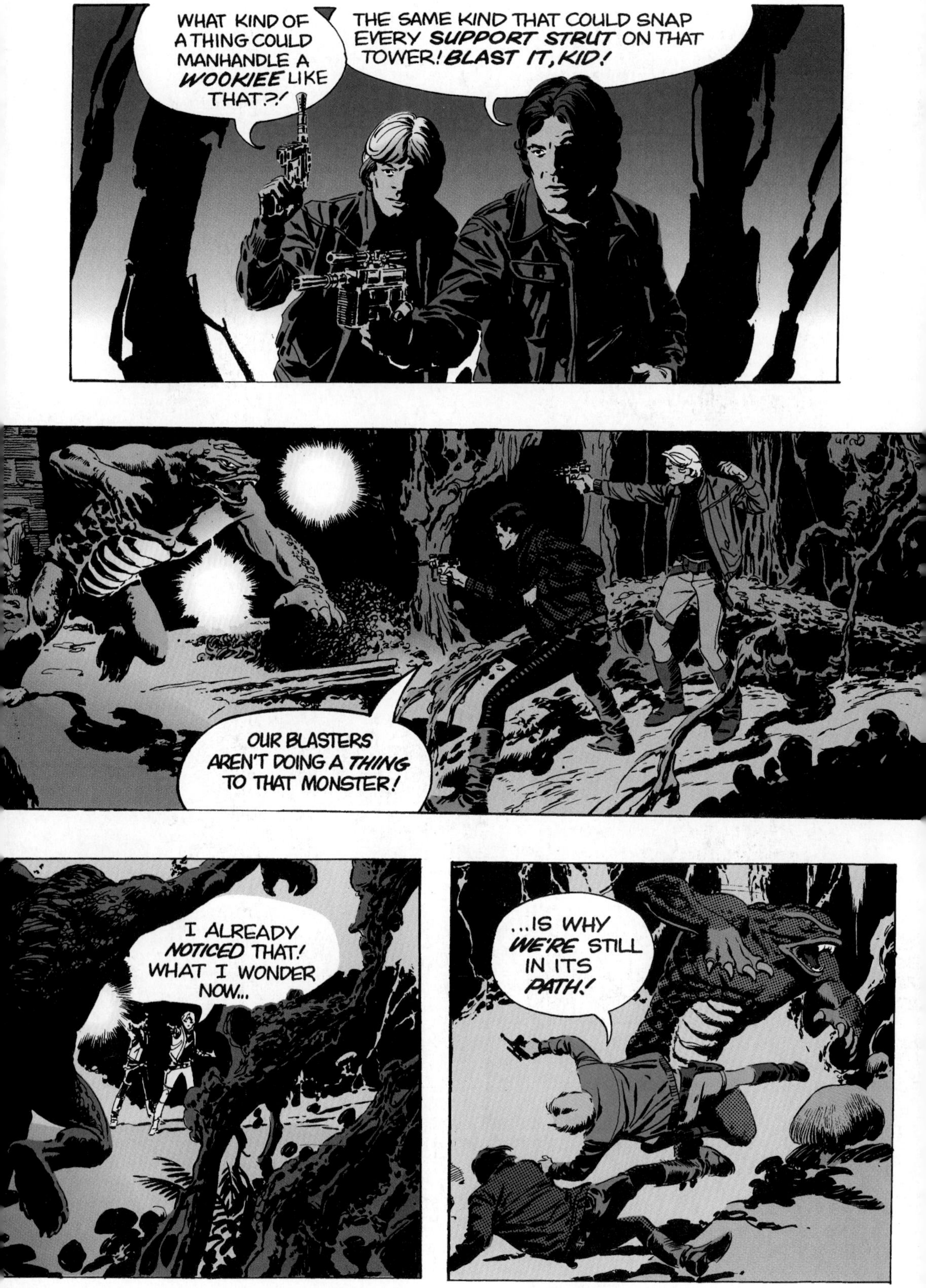
WHAT KIND OF A THING COULD MANHANDLE A *WOOKIEE* LIKE THAT?!
THE SAME KIND THAT COULD SNAP EVERY *SUPPORT STRUT* ON THAT TOWER! *BLAST IT, KID!*
OUR BLASTERS AREN'T DOING A *THING* TO THAT MONSTER!
I ALREADY *NOTICED* THAT! WHAT I WONDER NOW...
...IS WHY *WE'RE* STILL IN ITS *PATH!*

WE'LL NEVER DODGE IT A *SECOND* TIME-- IT'S TOO *FAST!*

But... IT DIDN'T *TURN* FOR US! IT'S JUST RUSHING ON...

STRAIGHT FOR THE *MAIN BUILDING* OF OUR *BASE!*

C'MON, CHEWIE! YOU MAY YET GET A *REMATCH* WITH THE THING THAT *TOSSED* YOU THERE!

MASTER LUKE! CAPTAIN SOLO! CHEWBACCA! THANK THE MAKER YOU'VE COME! SOMETHING *TERRIBLE* IS LOOSE IN THE MAIN HANGAR!

HAN, IT LOOKS LIKE A FLIGHT OF *TIE FIGHTERS* WENT THROUGH HERE!

I'D *PREFER* THAT, KID-- AT LEAST THEY'RE VULNERABLE TO *BLASTERS!*

WATCHING THAT CREATURE SHRUG OFF OUR FIRE WAS *SCARY*, ALL RIGHT. AND I GOT A FUNNY FEELING--

NAARGHH!

SAVE IT, LUKE! CHEWIE'S SNIFFED OUT *SOMETHING* IN THE SHADOWS OVER THERE!

DON'T *S-SHOOT*, SKYWALKER! IT'S ME! WE TRIED TO *S-STOP* THAT THING...

EASY, SIR! WE'LL GET MEDICAL DROIDS FOR YOU AND YOUR MEN!

H-HEARD THE CREATURE RAMPAGING... TURNED ON THE HANGAR LIGHTS... IT WENT *B-BERSERK!*

BUT NO SIGN OF IT *NOW.* IF IT RAN BACK OUTSIDE...

WE'D HAVE *SEEN* IT AS WE *APPROACHED*, HAN! THAT MEANS--

OUR MONSTER IS ROAMING *LOOSE* SOMEWHERE HERE IN REBEL HEADQUARTERS!

LATER...

LUKE...HOW'S THE SEARCH GOIN' ON *YOUR* LEVEL? CHEWIE'S TEAM DREW A *BLANK*. SAME WITH OUR OTHERS.

NOTHING, HAN. I'VE SENT MY MEN BACK TO REGULAR DUTY.

BLAST IT! IT RAMPAGED FROM THE FOREST INTO THE HANGAR AND DIDN'T COME *OUT!*

HOW CAN SOMETHING THAT *BIG* JUST DISAPPEAR.?!

SUPERSTITION ISN'T PART OF MY PROGRAMMING, SIR ... BUT AREN'T THERE MONSTERS IN HUMAN LEGEND THAT *VANISH* WITH *SUNRISE?*

A STRANGE END TO A STRANGE NIGHT...

GONE! WITHOUT A *TRACE!* A MONSTER BIG ENOUGH TO GIVE *CHEWIE* AN INFERIORITY COMPLEX.!

THE PLACE HAS BEEN THOROUGHLY *SEARCHED,* HAN. THE ROOF IS THE LAST--

SOMETHIN' RAMPAGED THROUGH THE MAIN HANGAR...

...UNLESS WE ALL HAD A *COLLECTIVE NIGHTMARE!*

AS I SUGGESTED EARLIER, SIR, PERHAPS THIS INVOLVES WHAT YOU HUMANS CALL....*THE SUPERNATURAL!*

KID, IS THIS TINPLATED TROUBLEMAKER *SERIOUSLY* SUGGESTING WE FOUGHT A *GHOST* LAST NIGHT?

YOU MAY LAUGH, CAPTAIN SOLO, BUT ONCE EVERYTHING *POSSIBLE* IS ELIMINATED...

...ONLY THE *IMPOSSIBLE* REMAINS!

LISTEN, GOLDENROD...! MAYBE LUKE AND OLD BEN KENOBI...

...GAVE ME SECOND THOUGHTS ABOUT THE *FORCE* BEIN' MUMBO-JUMBO, BUT *NOTHIN'S* GONNA MAKE ME BELIEVE--

HAN, THAT'S A POSSIBILITY WE *HAVEN'T* ELIMINATED!

LUKE... *LUKE!* WHERE YOU *GOIN'*?!

YOUR REMARK ABOUT THE *FORCE* SEEMS TO HAVE TRIGGERED SOMETHING, CAPTAIN...!

IF *THAT'S* CONNECTED WITH THE MYSTERY CREATURE... PERHAPS IT ISN'T *TRULY* EVIL!

WHAT ABOUT THE FORCE'S *DARK SIDE*? OR IS *DARTH VADER* JUST MISUNDERSTOOD?

The Rebel base's main hangar...

WHEN HAN AND I FOUGHT THE CREATURE AND OUR BLASTERS HAD NO EFFECT... I *FELT* SOMETHING... JUST BRIEFLY...

...SOMETHING LIKE... THE *FORCE* AT WORK!

GOODWIN AND WILLIAMSON

GOTTA REACH OUT WITH MY *FEELINGS* LIKE *BEN* TAUGHT ME...

MAYBE HERE... WHEN THE THING *VANISHED*...ALONE, CONCENTRATING... I CAN FEEL IT *AGAIN!*

But from the hangar's shadows...Luke is *WATCHED!*

IF THERE'S ANY CONNECTION BETWEEN THE *FORCE* AND THAT *CREATURE,* SURELY, I'LL *SENSE* IT AND...AND...

IT'S NO USE! I'M *TRYING* TOO HARD... *NOTHIN'S* HAPPENING!

HAN SOLO! A *MONSTER* AT LARGE ON THIS BASE AND YOU LET *LUKE* RUN OFF ALONE?!

HE MANAGED TO BLOW UP THE *DEATH STAR* ALONE, PRINCESS...

...AND AGAINST A CREATURE THAT SHRUGS OFF BLASTER FIRE AND SEEMINGLY *DISAPPEARS* AT WILL, I DOUBT I'D MAKE MUCH *DIFFERENCE*...

"...PARTICULARLY SINCE THE KID SEEMS TO BE TESTING *SOMETHIN'* INVOLVING THE *FORCE*."

I *THOUGHT* THERE WAS A *TRACE* WHEN WE FIRST *FOUGHT* THE THING!

NOW WE KNOW HOW OUR NIGHT BEAST SEEMINGLY *VANISHED!* BUT THERE'S *SOME* ASPECT OF THE FORCE ABOUT IT! I CAN FEEL--

A *WARNING BLEEP* sounds from the hangar shadows... but not in time to *STOP* the young warrior as he steps into darkness!

BUH-DOOOP!

ARTOO-DETOO....! DON'T TRY TO *FOLLOW* ME...THAT STONE'S *SLAMMING SHUT!*

The great stone slides back into place! Followed by *PITCH DARKNESS* and...

SKREEEEET!

Then...

DON'T *PANIC,* ARTOO! LOOKS LIKE YOU SQUEEZED IN SAFELY...WITH AT LEAST A *MICRO-CHIP'S WIDTH* TO SPARE!

By the light of an illumni-rod, Luke and his droid explore the secret underground corridor...

GLAD YOU WERE IN THE HANGAR KEEPING AN *EYE* ON ME, LITTLE GUY...THIS DOESN'T SEEM LIKE A FUN PLACE TO EXPLORE *ALONE!*

BRITTA VOOT DLEEP!

SORRY, ARTOO...*THIS* WAY...GOING BACK FOR HAN AND THE OTHERS IS TEMPTING...

...BUT I'M NOT *EXPERIENCED* ENOUGH YET WITH THE FORCE TO BE SURE I COULD GET US *IN* HERE AGAIN!

BESIDES... BEN KENOBI TAUGHT ME TO *FOLLOW* MY FEELINGS.

OF COURSE, IT MIGHT BE NICER IF THEY DIDN'T *LEAD* THE SAME DIRECTION A *MONSTER* TOOK.

AN *INTERSECTION!* THESE THINGS MUST CONNECT THE ENTIRE *MASSASSI RUINS!*

PROBABLY SOME KIND OF *SHELTER SYSTEM* FOR WHATEVER ANCIENT RACE OCCUPIED THE PLACE BEFORE THE *REBEL ALLIANCE!* MAYBE--

ARTOO! THERE'S *SOMETHING* DOWN THIS ONE!

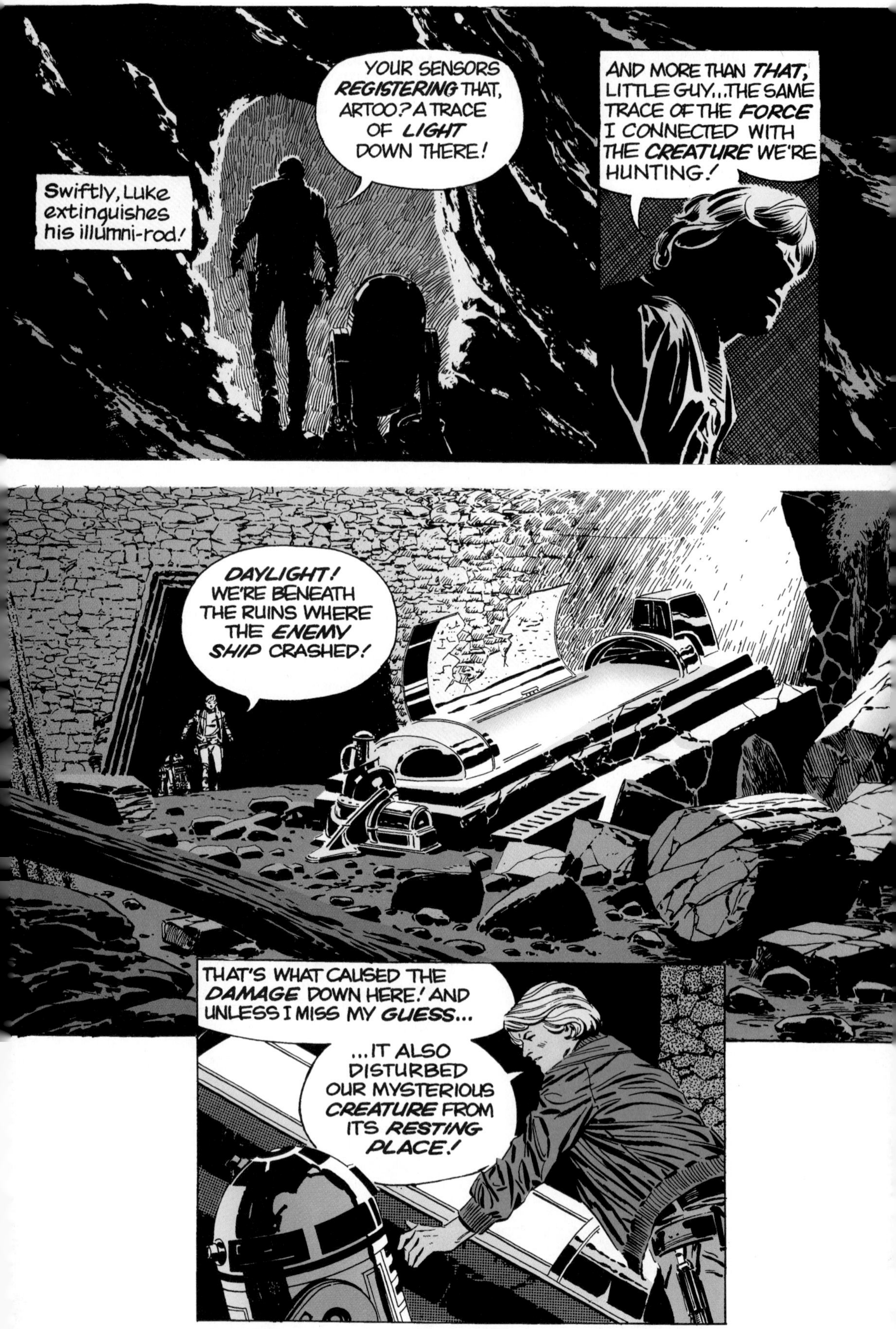
YOUR SENSORS REGISTERING THAT, ARTOO? A TRACE OF LIGHT DOWN THERE!
AND MORE THAN THAT, LITTLE GUY... THE SAME TRACE OF THE FORCE I CONNECTED WITH THE CREATURE WE'RE HUNTING!
Swiftly, Luke extinguishes his illumni-rod!
DAYLIGHT! WE'RE BENEATH THE RUINS WHERE THE ENEMY SHIP CRASHED!
THAT'S WHAT CAUSED THE DAMAGE DOWN HERE! AND UNLESS I MISS MY GUESS...
...IT ALSO DISTURBED OUR MYSTERIOUS CREATURE FROM ITS RESTING PLACE!

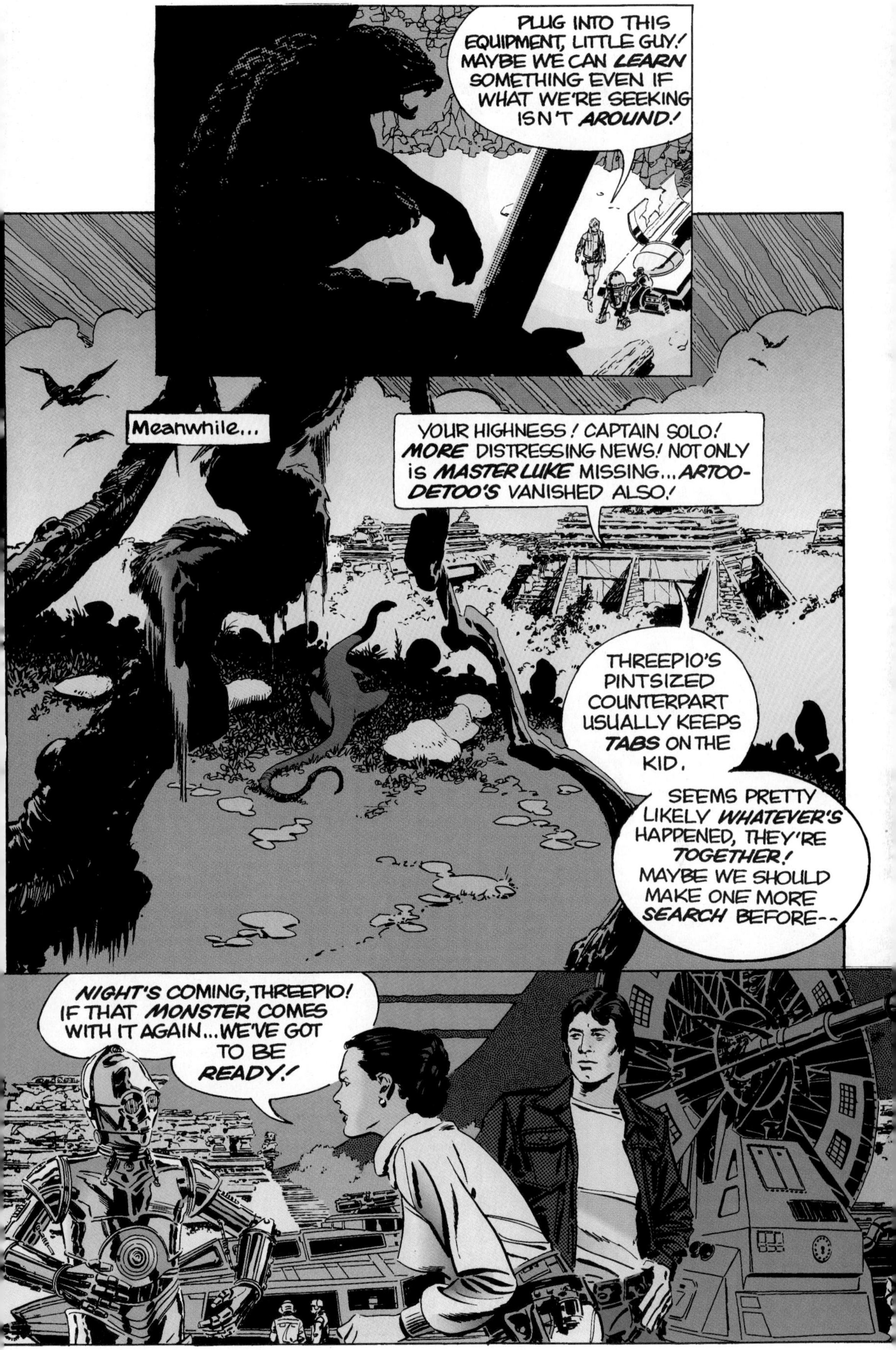
PLUG INTO THIS EQUIPMENT, LITTLE GUY! MAYBE WE CAN LEARN SOMETHING EVEN IF WHAT WE'RE SEEKING ISN'T AROUND!
Meanwhile...
YOUR HIGHNESS! CAPTAIN SOLO! MORE DISTRESSING NEWS! NOT ONLY is MASTER LUKE MISSING... ARTOO-DETOO'S VANISHED ALSO!
THREEPIO'S PINTSIZED COUNTERPART USUALLY KEEPS TABS ON THE KID.
SEEMS PRETTY LIKELY WHATEVER'S HAPPENED, THEY'RE TOGETHER! MAYBE WE SHOULD MAKE ONE MORE SEARCH BEFORE--
NIGHT'S COMING, THREEPIO! IF THAT MONSTER COMES WITH IT AGAIN... WE'VE GOT TO BE READY!

I DON'T LIKE JUST *FORGETTING* ABOUT THE KID, LEIA...

THINK *I* DO, HAN SOLO?! I'M NOT ADVOCATING ABANDONING OUR SEARCH FOR LUKE... BUT THIS IS MORE IMPORTANT.

WOOTA VRRRT-BLIP!

THAT MEANS YOU'RE *GETTING* SOMETHING FROM THIS EQUIPMENT'S *PROGRAMMING CIRCUITS*, ARTOO?

STUFF'S DAMAGED AND PRETTY ANCIENT... BUT IF IT CAN TELL US *WHY* THE BUILDERS OF THE MASSASSI RUINS LEFT THAT *CREATURE* HERE...

...MAYBE WE'LL HAVE A CLUE HOW TO *FIGHT* IT!

A chill *SNARL* interrupts Luke and Artoo!

HEAD BACK THE WAY WE *CAME*, LITTLE GUY!

ANY INFORMATIO YOU GOT *HAS* TO BE SAVED...

...I'LL DRAW THIS THING AFTER *ME!*

Reluctantly, Artoo follows orders, scooting in retreat down the ancient underground corridor...

...as Luke finds his *DIVERSION* all too successful!

THIS WAY WILL TAKE ME UP THROUGH THE RUINS TO THE *SURFACE*...

...EXCEPT THAT CREATURE CLIMBS A LOT *FASTER* OVER THESE BOULDERS THAN *I DO!*

THAT MONSTER WILL BE *ON* ME BEFORE I MAKE IT OUT OF THESE RUINS!

GOT TO *FIGHT!* AND SINCE BLASTERS HAVE NO *EFFECT* ON IT, THAT ONLY LEAVES...

...MY *LIGHTSABER!*

YOUR HIGHNESS... *LISTEN!* SNARLS AND CRIES FROM THE ABANDONED SECTION OF THE RUINS!

MUST BE OUR *NIGHT BEAST* LEIA! BUT WHAT COULD BE EXCITING IT *THERE?!*

Surprised by the night beast, Luke draws its pursuit to allow Artoo to escape! Climbing to the ruins above... he makes a *LAST STAND!*

BLASTERS HAVE NO EFFECT! ONLY HOPE IS...MY *LIGHTSABER!*

SEEMS TO MAKE IT *ANGRIER*... LASH OUT MORE *WILDLY!* THE *LIGHT!*

AFTER SLUMBERING SO LONG *UNDERGROUND* ANY STRONG LIGHT MUST DRIVE IT *BERSERK!* LIKE WHEN IT ATTACKED OUR *HANGAR!*

And as the creature's madly thrashing arms slam violently against the ancient structure's already weakened floor...

...*NEW COLLAPSE!*

His hand finds a hold! But...

VINE'S GONNA *BREAK*...DROP ME RIGHT INTO THE CREATURE'S *LAP!*

As the vine Luke clings to *SNAPS*...

ROWWRK!

CHEWIE! HAN! HOW?

YOU RAISED ENOUGH *NOISE* FIGHTIN' THAT CREATURE WE HEARD IT OVER AT THE MAIN BASE...DECIDED TO INVESTIGATE!

YOU'VE *SOLVED* OUR MONSTER PROBLEM, KID...NO WAY OUR UGLY-TEMPERED FRIEND CAN CLIMB FROM THERE NOW!

HE DOESN'T *HAVE* TO!

THERE ARE *HIDDEN TUNNELS* CONNECTING ALL THE BUILDINGS OF THE RUINS, HAN...PROBABLY PART OF A SHELTER SYSTEM BUILT BY MASSASSI'S ORIGINAL RESIDENTS!

AND OUR NIGHT BEAST *USED* ONE FOR HIS DISAPPEARING ACT.?

HE CAN *ALSO* USE THEM TO *REAPPEAR...* ANYWHERE HE WANTS!

MAKES A *DEFENSE* PRETTY IMPOSSIBLE! *BLAST IT!* GOTTA BE *SOME* WAY TO FIGHT THAT THING!

MAYBE THERE *IS...* IF I CAN FIND *ARTOO-DETOO!*

LUKE! WHAT'S *HAPPENING?* WHERE HAVE YOU BE--

NOT *NOW,* YOUR WORSHIP! THE KID'S GOTTA DO SOME FAST AND FANCY EVOKING OF THE *FORCE!*

ON A *BLANK WALL?!*

A wall with a section that *MOVES...*

THAT'S A *TUNNEL* BACK THERE, HAN! A-AND *SOMETHING'S* IN IT!

STAY *BACK,* LEIA... UNTIL WE'RE SURE *WHAT!*

VEETA BRIP WHR-DOOOT!

ARTOO... *GREAT!* YOU GOT BACK THROUGH THE TUNNELS JUST LIKE I *TOLD* YOU TO DO!

NOW LET'S SEE IF YOUR TAPPING THE MEMORY CIRCUITS OF THAT *EQUIPMENT* IN THE NIGHT BEAST'S *RESTING SPOT* NETTED ANYTHING TO *HELP* US!

And...

APPARENTLY TRANSLATION IS A PROBLEM, LUKE, BUT WITH *THREEPIO'S* EXPERTISE, WE'LL SURELY GET SOMETHING --

PRINCESS! MASTER LUKE! YOU'D BEST *SEE* THIS FOR *YOURSELVES!*

WHAT DID ARTOO *TURN UP* FROM THAT MACHINE? IT LOOKED *AGES* OLD!

ER...YOU AND MASTER LUKE JUST WATCH THE *SCREEN*, YOUR HIGHNESS!

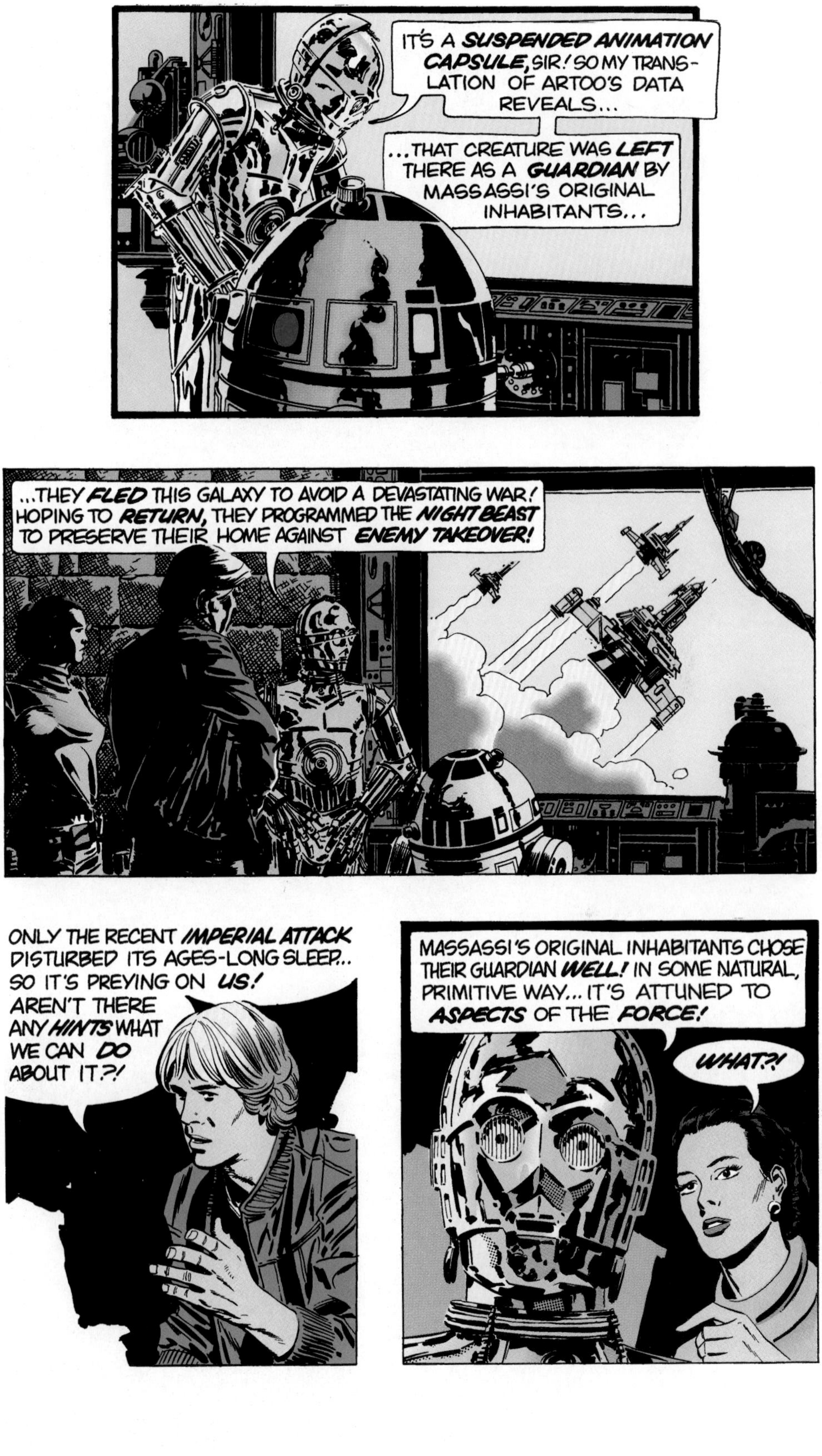
IT'S A SUSPENDED ANIMATION CAPSULE, SIR! SO MY TRANSLATION OF ARTOO'S DATA REVEALS...
...THAT CREATURE WAS LEFT THERE AS A GUARDIAN BY MASSASSI'S ORIGINAL INHABITANTS...
...THEY FLED THIS GALAXY TO AVOID A DEVASTATING WAR! HOPING TO RETURN, THEY PROGRAMMED THE NIGHT BEAST TO PRESERVE THEIR HOME AGAINST ENEMY TAKEOVER!
ONLY THE RECENT IMPERIAL ATTACK DISTURBED ITS AGES-LONG SLEEP... SO IT'S PREYING ON US! AREN'T THERE ANY HINTS WHAT WE CAN DO ABOUT IT?!
MASSASSI'S ORIGINAL INHABITANTS CHOSE THEIR GUARDIAN WELL! IN SOME NATURAL, PRIMITIVE WAY... IT'S ATTUNED TO ASPECTS OF THE FORCE!
WHAT?!

THREEPIO'S *RIGHT,* LEIA. I *SENSED* IT EARLIER.

BUT...ONLY *JEDI KNIGHTS* CAN MASTER THE FORCE!

MASTERY ISN'T *INVOLVED,* YOUR HIGHNESS... ONLY *SELF-PRESERVATION!* UNDER ATTACK, THE CREATURE MERELY *SHIELDS* ITSELF WITH THE FORCE BY INSTINCT!

WHICH MAKES IT "MERELY" *INVULNERABLE!*

THREEPIO, IS THAT *ALL* THE INFORMATION ARTOO'S TAP DREW FROM THE NIGHT BEAST'S SUSPENDED ANIMATION CAPSULE?

ANCIENT MEMORY CIRCUITS HAVE THEIR *LIMITS,* SIR...

AT LEAST WE KNOW THE CREATURE ISN'T TRULY *EVIL*...JUST UNABLE TO UNDERSTAND WE ARE NOT THE *ENEMY* IT'S PROGRAMMED TO DRIVE OUT!

SMALL CONSOLATION...

...WHEN IT CAN INSTINCTIVELY USE THE *FORCE* AS A SHIELD AGAINST ANY ATTACK! OUR DEFENSES CAN'T--

LEIA! LUKE! *COMPANY'S* ARRIVED...BIG AN' *UNFRIENDLY!*

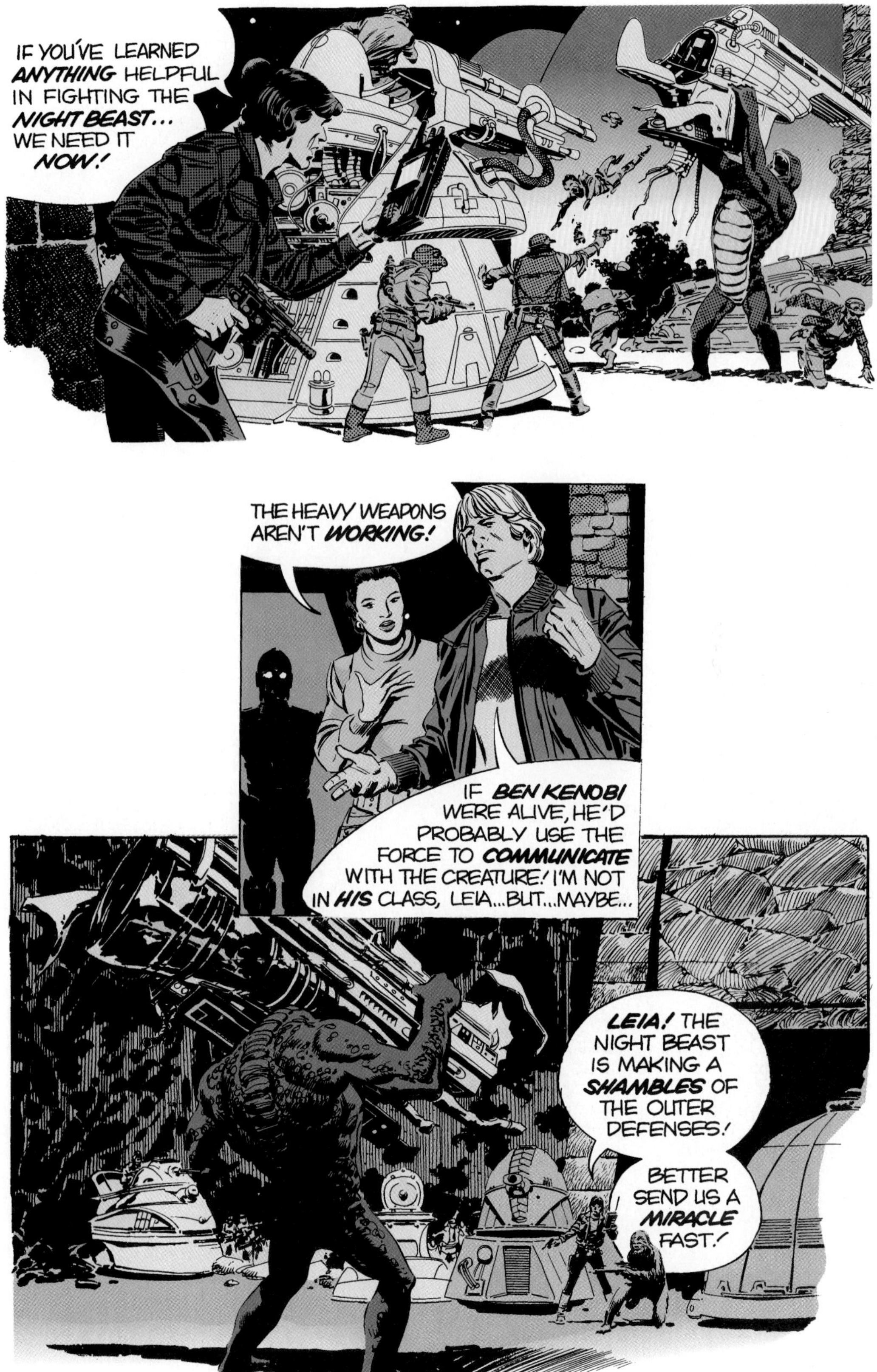

IF YOU'VE LEARNED ANYTHING HELPFUL IN FIGHTING THE NIGHT BEAST... WE NEED IT NOW!
THE HEAVY WEAPONS AREN'T WORKING!
IF BEN KENOBI WERE ALIVE, HE'D PROBABLY USE THE FORCE TO COMMUNICATE WITH THE CREATURE! I'M NOT IN HIS CLASS, LEIA...BUT...MAYBE...
LEIA! THE NIGHT BEAST IS MAKING A SHAMBLES OF THE OUTER DEFENSES!
BETTER SEND US A MIRACLE FAST!

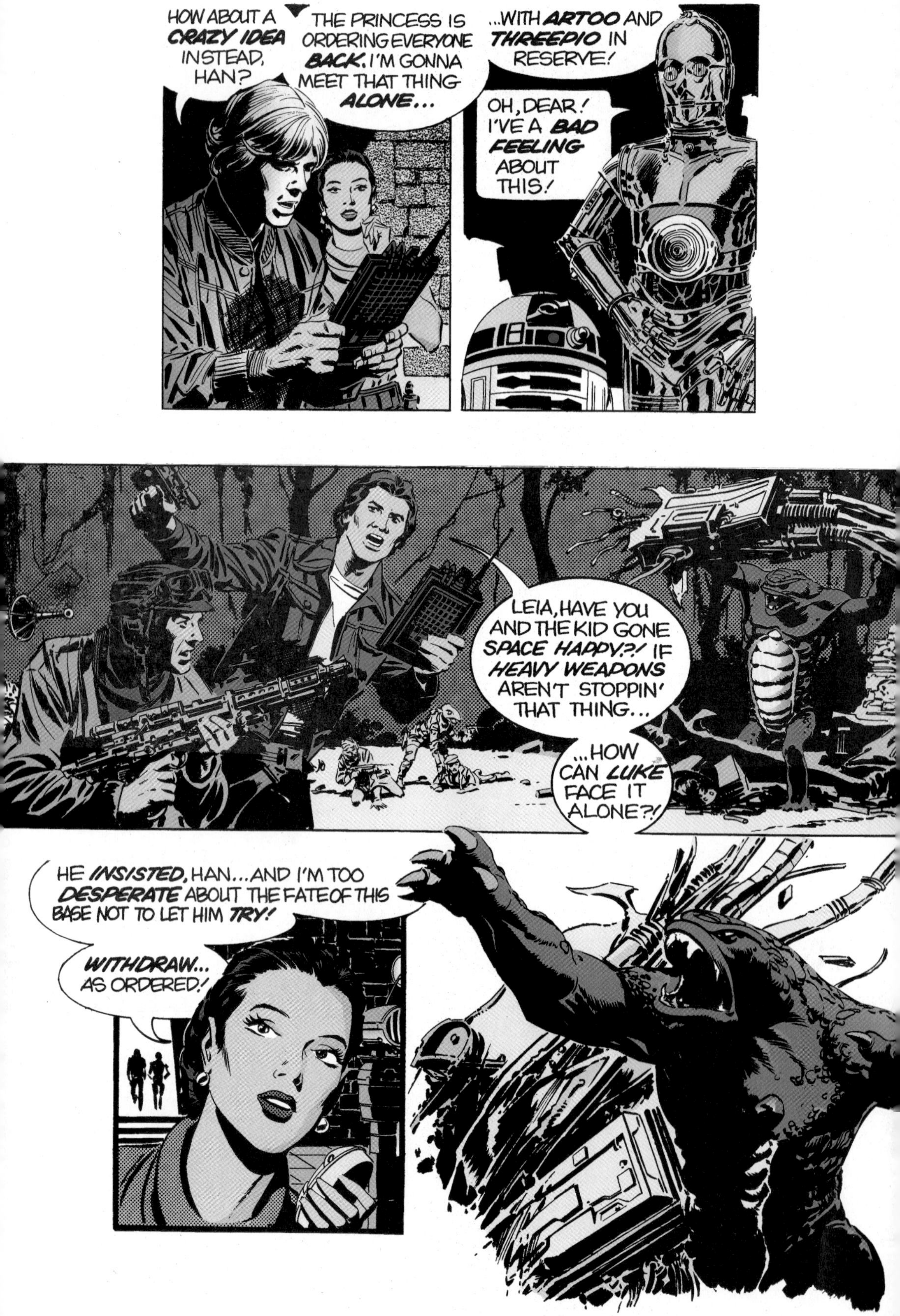
HOW ABOUT A CRAZY IDEA INSTEAD, HAN?
THE PRINCESS IS ORDERING EVERYONE BACK. I'M GONNA MEET THAT THING ALONE...
...WITH ARTOO AND THREEPIO IN RESERVE!
OH, DEAR! I'VE A BAD FEELING ABOUT THIS!
LEIA, HAVE YOU AND THE KID GONE SPACE HAPPY?! IF HEAVY WEAPONS AREN'T STOPPIN' THAT THING...
...HOW CAN LUKE FACE IT ALONE?!
HE INSISTED, HAN... AND I'M TOO DESPERATE ABOUT THE FATE OF THIS BASE NOT TO LET HIM TRY!
WITHDRAW... AS ORDERED!

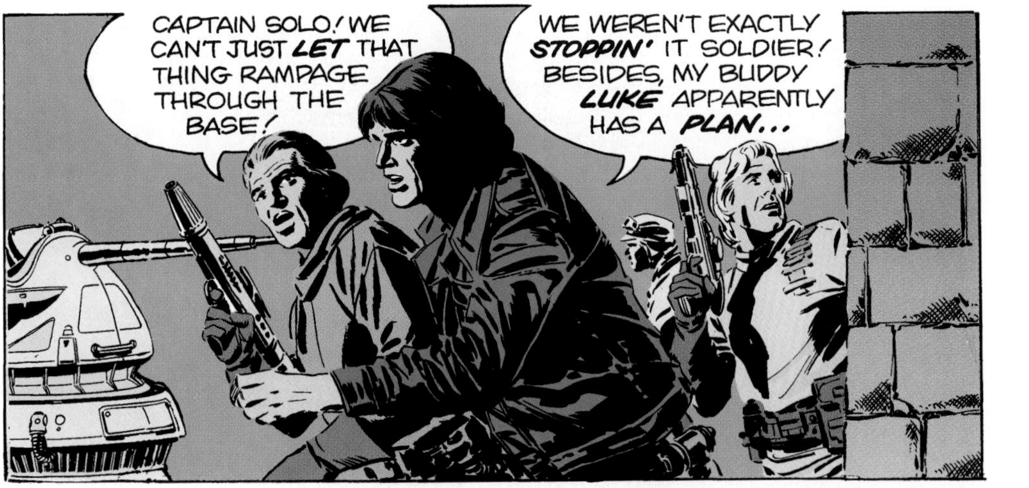
CAPTAIN SOLO! WE CAN'T JUST LET THAT THING RAMPAGE THROUGH THE BASE!
WE WEREN'T EXACTLY STOPPIN' IT SOLDIER! BESIDES, MY BUDDY LUKE APPARENTLY HAS A PLAN...

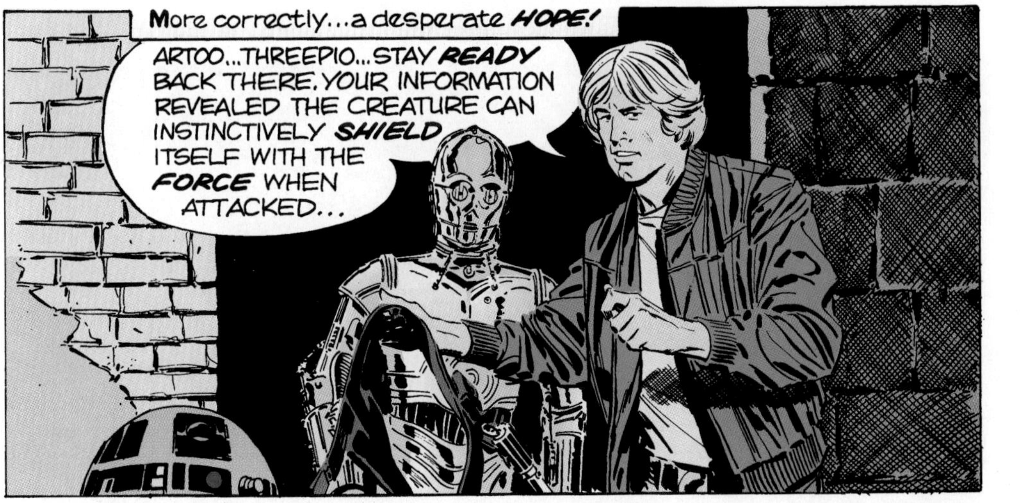
More correctly...a desperate HOPE!
ARTOO...THREEPIO...STAY READY BACK THERE. YOUR INFORMATION REVEALED THE CREATURE CAN INSTINCTIVELY SHIELD ITSELF WITH THE FORCE WHEN ATTACKED...

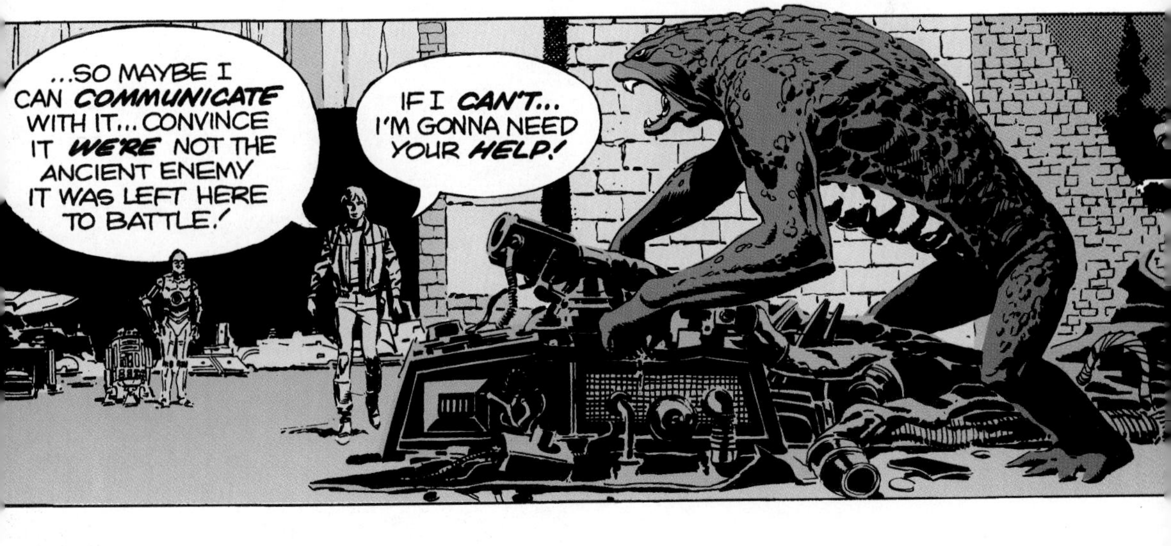
...SO MAYBE I CAN COMMUNICATE WITH IT... CONVINCE IT WE'RE NOT THE ANCIENT ENEMY IT WAS LEFT HERE TO BATTLE!
IF I CAN'T... I'M GONNA NEED YOUR HELP!

IF IT SEES I DON'T *INTEND* TO ATTACK... MAYBE IT'LL GIVE ME TIME TO REACH OUT WITH THE *FORCE* AND *COMMUNICATE!*

The creature's response...a savage *GROWL* and lunge *FORWARD!*

THREEPIO! ARTOO! GET READY!

YOU'RE MY *LAST HOPE* FOR COMMUNICATING WITH THIS *MONSTER!*

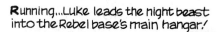

Running...Luke leads the night beast into the Rebel base's main hangar!

THREEPIO! TELL ARTOO TO START *TRANSMITTING...* NOW!

And suddenly the hangar's giant com-screen *GLOWS* with images...

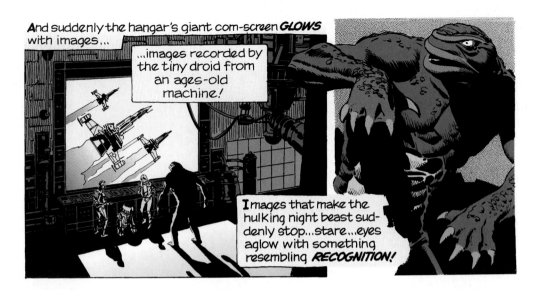

...images recorded by the tiny droid from an ages-old machine!

Images that make the hulking night beast suddenly stop...stare...eyes aglow with something resembling *RECOGNITION!*

SIR! IT'S *WORKING!* THE NIGHT BEAST SEEMS TO *RECOGNIZE* THIS AS THE DEPARTURE OF ITS *ORIGINAL MASTERS!*

Luke does not hear. With the creature momentarily calm, he is trying to reach out...

...reach out with the *FORCE.*

And suddenly, the monster whirls toward Luke... howling and snarling!

The night beast stalks after Luke... into a Rebel supply ship!

THE RAMP DOOR IS *SEALING!* MASTER LUKE IS *TRAPPED* WITH THAT MONSTER, ARTOO!

THREEPIO! HAVE A GROUND CREW MOVE THIS OUT FOR AN AUTO-PROGRAMMED *TAKE-OFF!*

SIR... YOU *OUTWITTED* THE CREATURE!

NO! I TOUCHED ITS MIND ENOUGH TO SEE IT WAS HOWLING IN *LONELINESS*...AND SHOWED IT A WAY TO *FOLLOW* WHERE ITS *ORIGINAL MASTERS* WENT.

ONCE I *REACHED* THE NIGHT BEAST WITH THE *FORCE*, THREEPIO... IT SEEMED TO *RECOGNIZE* I WASN'T THE ANCIENT ENEMY IT WAS LEFT HERE TO BATTLE.

THEN IT WENT *WILLINGLY* INTO THE SHIP, SIR? AS A WAY TO *FIND* ITS ORIGINAL MASTERS?

AND HOPEFULLY... SOMEWHERE OUT THERE IN THE STARS...IT *WILL!*

PART 10

"We know the *DIRECTION* they went," says Luke, "and the night beast wants to follow. Maybe somewhere among all those stars... he'll *FIND* them again.'"

LUKE? WHAT'S *WRONG*?

WHY DID YOU RUSH OUT? I WAS JUST--

GIVING ME CREDIT FOR USING THE *FORCE* TO HELP US OUT OF THIS LAST SCRAPE!

FACT IS...I JUST GOT *LUCKY*, LEIA! BUMBLED MY WAY THROUGH! BEN KENOBI AWAKENED THIS GREAT *POWER* IN ME...

...BUT HE'S *GONE* NOW! I DON'T KNOW WHAT I'M *DOING!*

I *MISS* BEN... AND NEED HIS *HELP* MORE THAN EVER!

OBI-WAN KENOBI WAS A GREAT MAN, LUKE. I *UNDERSTAND* HOW YOU MUST MISS HIM.

YOU'VE LOST EVEN *MORE*, LEIA. YOUR FATHER... YOUR ENTIRE HOME PLANET.

IT'S JUST...SOMETIMES I FEEL BEN'S STILL *WITH* US! IF ONLY I KNEW THE PROPER WAY TO REACH OUT... TO *FIND* HIM!

Meanwhile...

LORD VADER? TRANSMISSION FROM ADMIRAL GRIFF IN CHARGE OF OUR REBEL BLOCKADE. HE CLAIMS IT'S *URGENT!*

THE REBELS HAVE GATHERED *ALLIES* TO THEIR YAVIN BASE, LORD VADER... OUR BLOCKADE IS *INEFFECTIVE!* WE MUST--

LAUNCH A *FULL-SCALE ATTACK,* GRIFF?

IT'S THE *ONLY* LOGICAL COURSE!

TAKEN AT *MY* PACE, ADMIRAL... NOT *YOURS!* WHEN MY *STAR DESTROYER* IS READY... AND CERTAIN *OTHER EVENTS* ARE IN MOTION!

LORD VADER, EACH DAY WE DELAY, THE MORE *ALLIES* THE REBELS GATHER TO THEIR YAVIN BASE!

THE MORE TO BE CRUSHED *LATER,* GRIFF.

On the harsh, desert world of *ARIDUS,* an Imperial patrol closes in on its prey...

THAT'S THE CAMP! TIME TO *ELIMINATE* ONE REBEL WEAPONS SMUGGLER... AND HIS *CUSTOMERS!*

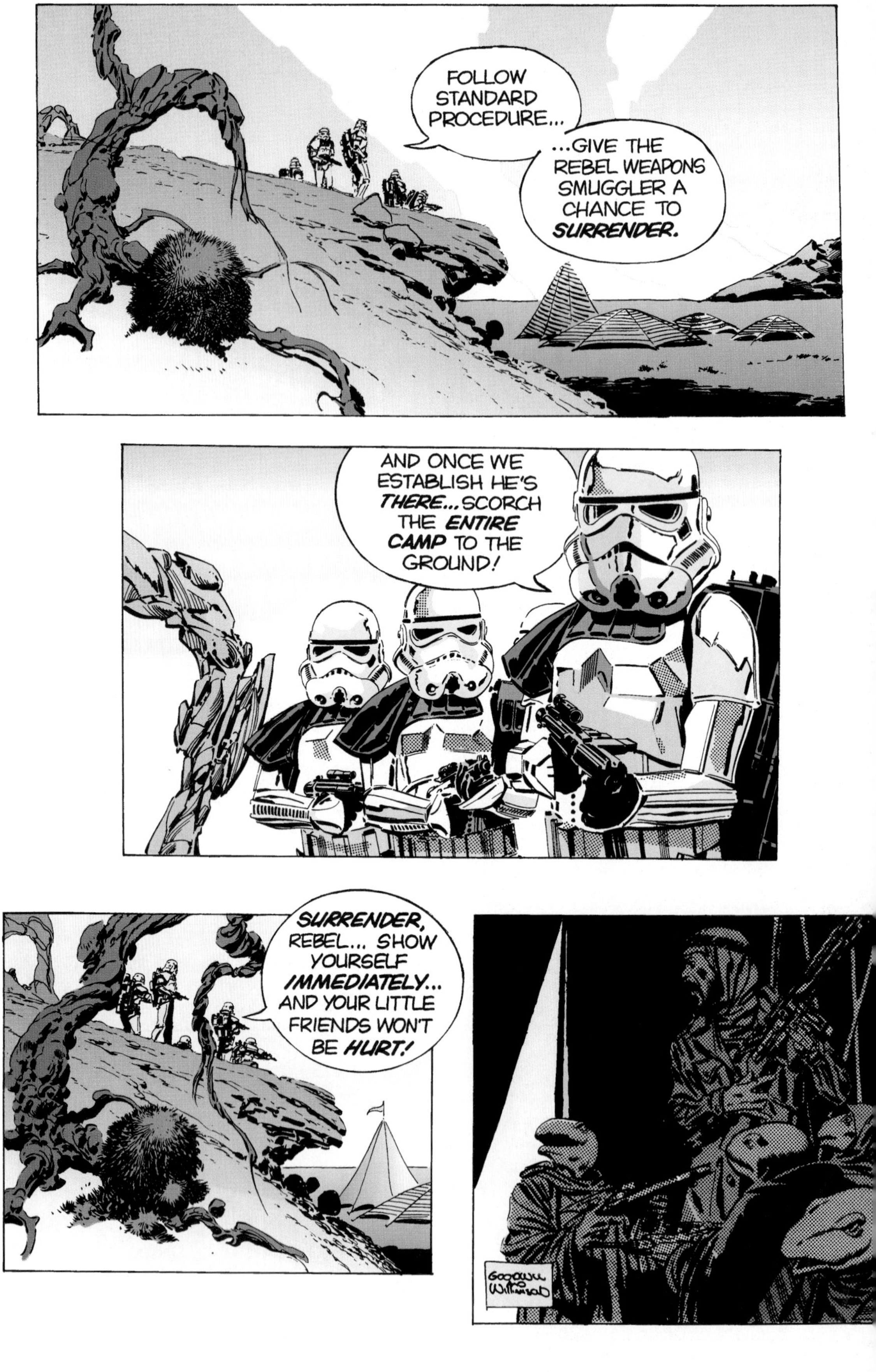
FOLLOW STANDARD PROCEDURE...
...GIVE THE REBEL WEAPONS SMUGGLER A CHANCE TO *SURRENDER.*
AND ONCE WE ESTABLISH HE'S *THERE...* SCORCH THE *ENTIRE CAMP* TO THE GROUND!
SURRENDER, REBEL... SHOW YOURSELF *IMMEDIATELY...* AND YOUR LITTLE FRIENDS WON'T BE *HURT!*

HE'S *FALLEN* FOR IT! IT'S SAFE TO *OBLITERATE* THE WHOLE CAMP!

NO!

About to fire... a *VOICE* makes the stormtroopers *TURN!*

YOU'RE *MEDDLING* IN THE *EMPIRE'S* BUSINESS, OLD MAN...

...GET *OUT* OR *DIE!*

INTERESTING. I WAS ABOUT TO SUGGEST THAT *YOU* DEPART.

While below...

SOMETHING'S *DISTRACTED* THE IMPERIALS... *RUN FOR IT! SCATTER!*

THE *REBEL* WEAPONS SMUGGLER AND HIS NATIVE CUSTOMERS ARE *GETTING AWAY!*

KILL THEM! I'LL FINISH THIS INTERFERING OLD *FOOL!*

MY FRIEND, YOU'RE *FORCING* ME INTO SOMETHING I HOPED TO *AVOID.*

And beneath the harsh desert sun of Aridus...

...a *LIGHTSABER* flashes!

For a brief instant, Imperial fire rakes the small encampment...

...only to be swiftly, suddenly *SILENCED!*

W-WHO... *ARE* YOU?!

SOME CALL ME... *BEN.*

BEN KENOBI.

YAVIN FOUR! Main base of the Rebel Alliance... ...a wounded agent returns from his mission.

YOU'RE *SURE* ABOUT WHAT HAPPENED ON *ARIDUS*?

OTHERWISE, I'D BE *DEAD,* SKYWALKER..

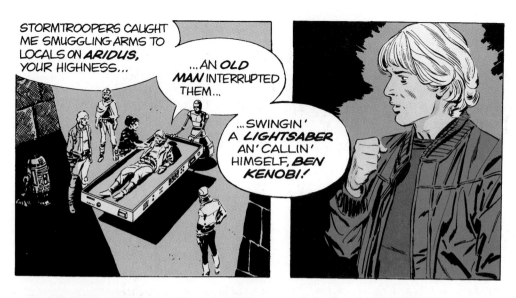

STORMTROOPERS CAUGHT ME SMUGGLING ARMS TO LOCALS ON *ARIDUS*, YOUR HIGHNESS...

...AN *OLD MAN* INTERRUPTED THEM...

...SWINGIN' A *LIGHTSABER* AN' CALLIN' HIMSELF, *BEN KENOBI!*

LUKE, THAT MAN'S *WOUNDED!* HE'S BEEN GIVEN *MEDICATION*...WHAT HE SAID ABOUT *BEN KENOBI* BEING ON *ARIDUS* *HAS* TO BE A...*DELUSION!*

Luke insists on resuming the Rebel weapons smuggler's mission...

LUKE, I *FORBID* THIS...THAT STORY *CAN'T* BE TRUE!

WEAPON DELIVERIES TO *ARIDUS* *HAVE* TO CONTINUE, LEIA...AND THIS IS *ONE* TRUTH *NO ONE* CAN JUDGE BETTER THAN *ME!*

YOU'RE DOING THIS FOR *YOURSELF*... NOT THE *ALLIANCE*!

I'VE *GOT* TO KNOW!

BUT IF BEN KENOBI'S REALLY *ALIVE*... HE COULD HELP US *ALL*, LEIA!

AND IF HIS APPEARANCE ON ARIDUS IS A LIE OR A MISTAKE...

...YOU COULD BE GOING INTO A *DEATHTRAP*!

THAT'S WHY I'M GOING *ALONE*!

HAN! CHEWBACCA! IF LUKE WON'T LISTEN TO *ME*... MAYBE *YOU* CAN STOP HIM!

NOT WITHOUT A *FIGHT*, YOUR ROYALNESS...

...AND I'M NOT SURE *ANYBODY* WOULD COME OUT OF THAT A WINNER!

SOME SITUATIONS EVEN A *PRINCESS* AND *REBEL LEADER* CAN'T DO MUCH ABOUT, LEIA...

...EXCEPT GRIT YOUR TEETH... AND WISH THE KID *WELL*!

Luke's smuggling ship leaps through hyperspace...bound for *ARIDUS!* Then...

THAT *BANGING!* SOUNDS LIKE SOMETHING'S BROKEN LOOSE IN THE CARGO HOLD!

THREEPIO?! I LEFT YOU DROIDS BACK AT THE BASE!

YOU *KNOW* HOW ARTOO-DETOO DISREGARDS ORDERS, SIR! I CAME ABOARD TO *PREVENT* HIS STOWING AWAY...

...AND FOUND OUT *TOO LATE* THAT THIS TIME HE'D *OBEYED* YOU!

THERE'S *NO LIMIT* TO THAT LITTLE RUSTPOT'S TROUBLEMAKING!

Luke makes a secret landing on *ARIDUS*...

JUST *LOOK*, THREEPIO... IT'S *GREAT!* IF THERE WERE TWO SUNS, I'D SWEAR I WAS BACK HOME ON *TATOOINE!*

OH, DEAR! DO THE NATIVES HERE INDULGE IN *DROID SELLING* LIKE THOSE NASTY LITTLE *JAWAS?!*

WE'LL LEARN WHEN WE *FIND* THEM, BUT-- *GET DOWN!*

Explosions rock the sands of Aridus!

MASTER LUKE...THOSE ARE *PROTON GRENADES!*

WE'VE *FOUND* THE LOCALS, THREEPIO!

THEY'RE TRYING TO ATTACK SOME MANNER OF *IMPERIAL HOVER-TRAIN* SIR!

AND IT'S TOO WELL *DEFENDED* FOR THEM TO SUCCEED!

NO *WONDER* THE NATIVES OF ARIDUS NEED *WEAPONS* FROM THE REBEL ALLIANCE, THREEPIO.

BUT IT APPEARS *OUR* SHIPMENT HAS ARRIVED *TOO LATE* TO HELP THEM, MASTER LUKE!

THEY NEED MORE *FIREPOWER* LIKE THE *PROTON CHARGES* WE BROUGHT WITH THE *OTHER* WEAPONS WE'RE SMUGGLING!

SIR, SURELY *WE'RE* NOT GETTING INTO THE BATTLE, ARE WE? *SIR?!*

22

OH, NO! WE *ARE!* ARTOO-DETOO, THIS IS ALL *YOUR* FAULT!

TRYING TO PREVENT *YOU* FROM STOWING AWAY IN MASTER LUKE'S SHIP... I GOT TRAPPED ABOARD *MYSELF!*

NOW, THREEPIO! WHILE THE IMPERIALS' ATTENTION IS STILL ON THE OTHER SIDE OF THE TRAIN... *THROW!*

SIR! IF ONE FALLS *SHORT...* WE'RE *DOOMED!*

MY ARMOR'S A *MESS* FROM *FLYING DEBRIS* AND --

MASTER *LUKE!*

I *KNEW* WE WERE TOO CLOSE WHEN WE THREW THOSE CHARGES INTO THE IMPERIALS' HOVER-TRAIN!

MASTER LUKE... *SIR!* TELL ME YOU'RE STILL *ALIVE!*

BEST NOT TO *MOVE* HIM TOO SUDDENLY...

...BUT HE ONLY APPEARS *STUNNED...* PERHAPS A SLIGHT CONCUSSION FROM THE FLYING DEBRIS.

AH...SEE? HE'S COMING AROUND.

TH-THAT VOICE ....*KNOW* ...THAT VOICE...

SHOO*!* *BACK!* DON'T YOU OVER-CURIOUS TWERPS KNOW BETTER THAN TO *CROWD* AN INJURED PERSON?

FRRR SZZZK!

I *UNDERSTOOD* THAT, YOU TINY BARBARIAN! I *AM* A TRANSLATOR DROID!

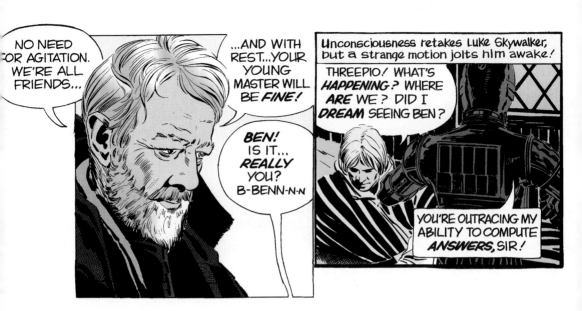

NO NEED FOR AGITATION. WE'RE ALL FRIENDS...

...AND WITH REST...YOUR YOUNG MASTER WILL BE *FINE!*

BEN! IS IT... *REALLY* YOU? B-BENN-N-N

Unconsciousness retakes Luke Skywalker, but a strange motion jolts him awake!

THREEPIO! WHAT'S *HAPPENING?* WHERE *ARE* WE? DID I *DREAM* SEEING BEN?

YOU'RE OUTRACING MY ABILITY TO COMPUTE *ANSWERS,* SIR!

WE'RE ON SOMETHING THE NATIVES OF ARIDUS CALL A *WIND-RUNNER...*

...AND IT'S CARRYING US TO REJOIN *OBI-WAN KENOBI!*

YOU SUFFERED A *NASTY BLOW* FROM FLYING DEBRIS WHEN WE BLEW UP THAT IMPERIAL HOVER-TRAIN!

THREEPIO, THERE'S NO *MISTAKE*? YOU SAW HIM TOO? *BEN KENOBI*... ALIVE? RIGHT HERE ON *ARIDUS*?

HE HAD TO MOVE ON IN A *HURRY*, MASTER LUKE...

...APPARENTLY HE'S ORGANIZING THE *CHUBBITS* -- THESE LOCAL DESERT DWELLERS -- TO RESIST THE IMPERIAL TAKEOVER!

I CAN'T *WAIT* FOR THIS *WIND-RUNNER* TO TAKE US TO *REJOIN* HIM!

Meanwhile...

LORD VADER! IT'S THE *TRANSMISSION* YOU'VE BEEN EXPECTING!

MAINTAIN *FULL SPEED*, CAPTAIN... AND SEE I'M NOT *DISTURBED* DURING THE TRANSMISSION!

OF *COURSE*, MY LORD!

THE YOUTH HAS MADE *CONTACT*, MY LORD...

...ALL IS PROCEEDING ACCORDING TO YOUR *PLAN*.

OF COURSE, HE ONLY GLIMPSED ME *BRIEFLY*. MY IMPERSONATION ISN'T *FULLY* TESTED.

DOUBT HAS NO PLACE IN MY PLAN!

LORD VADER, I DIDN'T MEAN TO IMPLY LACK OF *FAITH* IN YOUR PLAN.! IT'S JUST THAT THIS *SKYWALKER* SEEMS--

HE IS TOUCHED BY THE *FORCE.*

IT MAKES DECEPTION *DIFFICULT,* BUT OLD OBI-WAN-- THE MAN YOU IMPERSONATE-- HAD LITTLE TIME TO *TEACH* THE YOUTH...

SKYWALKER'S POWERS ARE *UNHONED!* GIVEN THAT, AND ALL I AND THE EMPIRE HAVE PROVIDED YOU... YOU *CANNOT* FAIL!

FORGIVE AN *ACTOR* MOMENTARY *STAGE-FRIGHT,* SIRE!

HEAR ME, ACTOR.! IMPERIAL SURGEONS HAVE MADE YOUR RESEMBLANCE TO OBI-WAN KENOBI *PERFECT...*

...*MY* TRAINING, PLUS SOME TECHNOLOGICAL TRICKERY, MAKES THAT RESEMBLANCE *MORE* THAN PHYSICAL!

YOU'VE GIVEN ME THE *ROLE* OF A LIFETIME, LORD VADER! I'M TRYING TO BE *WORTHY* OF IT!

THE CHUBBITS--ARIDUS'S LOCAL DESERT DWELLERS-- AND I HAVE JUST LAID WASTE TO AN *IMPERIAL OUTPOST,* LORD VADER...

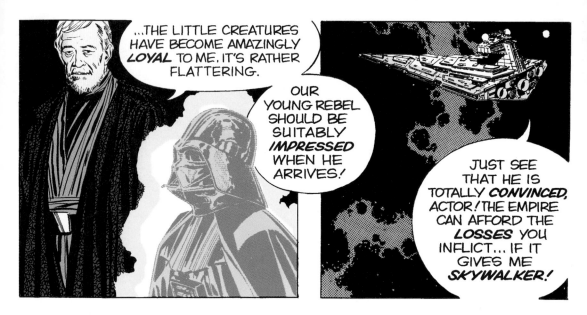

...THE LITTLE CREATURES HAVE BECOME AMAZINGLY *LOYAL* TO ME. IT'S RATHER FLATTERING.

OUR YOUNG REBEL SHOULD BE SUITABLY *IMPRESSED* WHEN HE ARRIVES!

JUST SEE THAT HE IS TOTALLY *CONVINCED*, ACTOR! THE EMPIRE CAN AFFORD THE *LOSSES* YOU INFLICT...IF IT GIVES ME *SKYWALKER!*

SSSST TZZZZ!

TIME TO BREAK OFF *COMMUNICATION*, LORD VADER...MY LITTLE ALLIES HAVE SPOTTED A *WIND-RUNNER* APPROACHING...

IT BRINGS *LUKE SKYWALKER!*

THEN I'LL SEE YOU BOTH *SOON*, ACTOR... AT THE *IRON TOWER!*

ANY CHANGE OF ORDERS, MY LORD?

SAME COURSE AT *FULL SPEED,* CAPTAIN. I WISH TO REACH ARIDUS IN *RECORD TIME!*

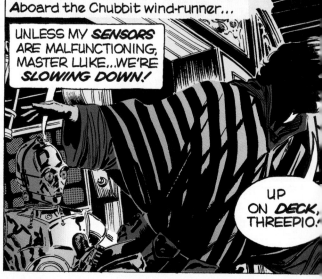

Aboard the Chubbit wind-runner...

UNLESS MY *SENSORS* ARE MALFUNCTIONING, MASTER LUKE...WE'RE *SLOWING DOWN!*

UP ON *DECK,* THREEPIO!

The Chubbit wind-runner rolls to a halt.

He *IS,...*or rather the man trained by *DARTH VADER* and altered by Imperial surgeons to *IMPERSONATE* him!

BEN! BEN!

Meanwhile, a supposedly "dead" enemy shows signs of life!

IS IT *REALLY* YOU? I BARELY *GLIMPSED* YOU BEFORE!

WE'LL HAVE MUCH TO *TALK* ABOUT NOW THAT YOU'VE RECOVERED FROM YOUR INJURY!

BEN!

Luke throws himself into the path of the dying stormtrooper's shot! But...

T-THE BLAST DIDN'T *TOUCH* US! BEN...YOU USED THE *FORCE* TO PROTECT US!

SO IT MUST *SEEM,* SKYWALKER...

RATHER, I ACTIVATED THE *MICRO-ENERGY SHIELD* PROVIDED ME BY IMPERIAL TECHNICIANS UNDER LORD VADER'S ORDERS!

SSSST ZLLSSK!

MASTER LUKE! THE CHUBBITS AND I HEARD A *SHOT!* ARE YOU *ALL RIGHT?!*

THANKS TO *BEN*...AND THE *FORCE,* THREEPIO!

I'VE HAD TROUBLE *BELIEVING* YOU SURVIVED BATTLING *DARTH VADER* ON THE DEATH STAR, BEN...

BUT AFTER SEEING THE WAY YOU *SHIELDED* US FROM THAT STORMTROOPER'S LAST BLAST... I'LL BELIEVE *ANYTHING!*

A *VICTORY* FOR LORD VADER...AND IMPERIAL TECHNOLOGY!

WHAT **NOW**, BEN? THE REBEL ALLIANCE CAN **REALLY** USE YOUR HELP AGAINST THE EMPIRE...

...AND NOT JUST ON A **BACKWATER** PLANET LIKE **ARIDUS!**

YOUR HOMEWORLD OF **TATOOINE** WAS SUCH A PLANET, LUKE...AS I RECALL SOME RATHER **MOMENTOUS EVENTS** BEGAN THERE.

YOU'RE **RIGHT**, BEN...AS ALWAYS! THANK THE FORCE I'VE GOT YOU FOR A **TEACHER** AGAIN!

STRANGE FEELING... BASKING IN THE **RESPECT** MEANT FOR **ANOTHER** MAN!

PERHAPS THE STRUGGLE AGAINST THE EMPIRE ON ARIDUS CAN BE ENDED **SWIFTLY**, LUKE...

I'LL DO **ANYTHING** YOU WANT, BEN!

THAT'S EXACTLY WHAT **LORD VADER** FELT, SKYWALKER!

WE'RE RIDING TO THE **IRON TOWER**, YOUNGSTER... JUST THE **TWO** OF US!

MASTER LUKE! YOU AND GENERAL KENOBI DON'T WANT ME TO *ACCOMPANY* YOU?

MY CHUBBIT FRIENDS WILL SEE THE DROID BACK TO YOUR *SHIP*, LUKE.

A *DECISIVE BLOW* CAN BE STRUCK THERE AGAINST THE IMPERIALS...BUT NOT IF WE'RE *ENCUMBERED* IN ANY WAY, LUKE!

Two riders move across the desert vastness of Aridus...

THIS IS JUST LIKE WHEN WE *MET* BACK ON TATOOINE, BEN...EXCEPT WE'RE RIDING *LIZARDS* INSTEAD OF MY OL' *LANDSPEEDER!*

I CAN'T TELL SKYWALKER THAT A DROID'S *SENSORS* MIGHT DETECT THE CONCEALED *CIRCUITRY* THAT ENABLES ME TO SIMULATE ASPECTS OF THE *FORCE*...

...SUCH AS THE *ENERGY SHIELD* WHICH SAVED US FROM THAT ATTACKING *STORMTROOPER!*

Meanwhile...

ARIDUS DEAD AHEAD, LORD VADER... AND IN RECORD TIME!

PREPARE A *LAUNCH*, CAPTAIN! I'VE A RENDEZVOUS... AT THE *IRON TOWER!*

ATMOSPHERIC CONDITIONS ON ARIDUS MAKE LONG-RANGE COMMUNICATION *IMPOSSIBLE*...

THE *IRON TOWER* IS SOMETHING THE EMPIRE BUILT TO *OVERCOME* THAT, BEN?

IT'S A GIGANTIC *POWER TRANSFORMER* AND *SIGNAL AMPLIFIER*, LUKE...TOTALLY AUTOMATED. WITHOUT IT... THEIR HOVER-TRAIN ORE TRANSPORT SYSTEM COULDN'T *FUNCTION.*

"BUT THE ULTRA-STRONG FREQUENCY OF ITS SIGNALS HAS A *DEVASTATING* EFFECT ON THE NATIVE CHUBBITS..."

"...CRIPPLING THEIR NERVOUS SYSTEMS... IN TIME, *FATALLY!*"

THE *IRON TOWER* IS THE GREATEST SYMBOL OF *IMPERIAL TYRANNY* ON ARIDUS! WHILE IT OPERATES... THE *CHUBBITS* ARE BEING STEADILY *DESTROYED!*

ARMED WITH THE *FORCE,* YOU AND I STAND A BETTER CHANCE AGAINST THE TOWER'S *AUTOMATED DEFENSES* THAN--

BEN...

...THERE ARE *OTHER* DEFENSES! WE'VE BEEN SPOTTED BY AN *IMPERIAL PATROL SPEEDER!*

THE IMPERIALS AREN'T INTERESTED IN ANYTHING BUT *BLASTING* ON SIGHT!

GET *AWAY*, BEN...! YOU STAND THE BEST CHANCE OF TACKLING THE *IRON TOWER* ALONE.'

...I'LL TRY TO *HOLD* 'EM.'

THIS IS THE *SECOND* TIME THE BOY'S BEEN WILLING TO *SACRIFICE* HIMSELF FOR ME.' INCREDIBLE HOW *DEEPLY* FEELINGS RUN FOR THE MAN I'M IMPERSONATING!

DARTH VADER INSPIRES LOYALTY THROUGH *FEAR*...BUT *NOTHING* APPROACHING THE FEELING *SKYWALKER* EXHIBITS FOR THE MAN *I'M* SUPPOSED TO BE.'

BEN! *RIDE* BEFORE THAT PATROL SPEEDER GETS ANY *CLOSER!*

I'LL FIGHT TO BUY YOU *TIME* TO REACH THE *IRON TOWER!* BUT IT'S GONNA TAKE--

...A...A *MIRACLE!*

DID YOU *SEE* THAT, BEN?

SOMEONE JUST *BLASTED* THAT IMPERIAL PATROL SPEEDER'S *MAIN THRUSTER!* IT'S OUT OF *CONTROL!*

THERE ARE *CHUBBITS* IN THE ROCKS BEHIND IT.*

SOME OF THEM MUST HAVE *DISOBEYED* YOUR ORDERS AND *FOLLOWED* US!

DEMONSTRATING THE SAME AFFECTION AND SELF-SACRIFICE *YOU'VE* SHOWN FOR BEN KENOBI, SKYWALKER!

IT'S MORE FLATTERING THAN ANY *APPLAUSE* I'VE DRAWN IN MY ACTING CAREER...BUT IT CAN'T STAND IN THE WAY OF MY TASK FOR *DARTH VADER!*

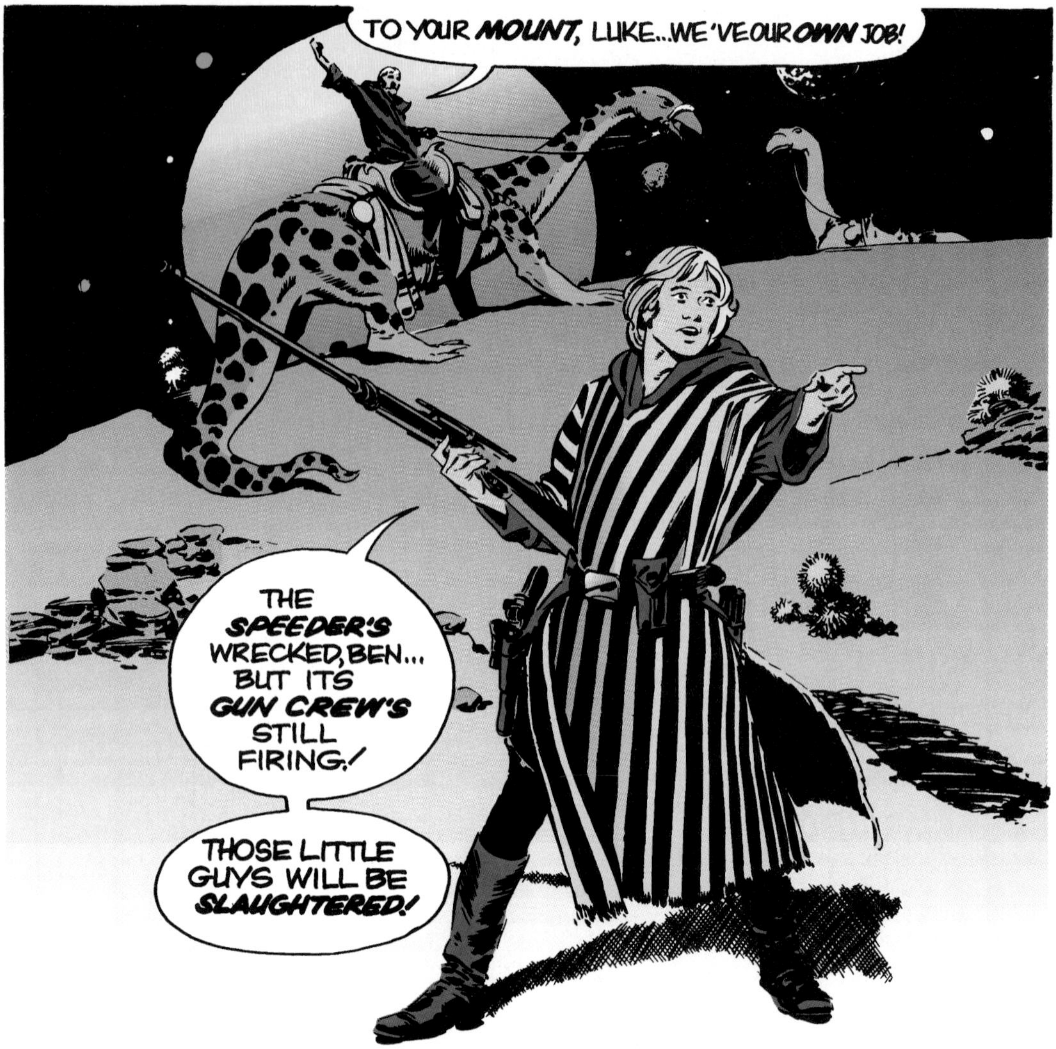
TO YOUR MOUNT, LUKE...WE'VE OUR OWN JOB!
THE SPEEDER'S WRECKED, BEN... BUT ITS GUN CREW'S STILL FIRING!
THOSE LITTLE GUYS WILL BE SLAUGHTERED!

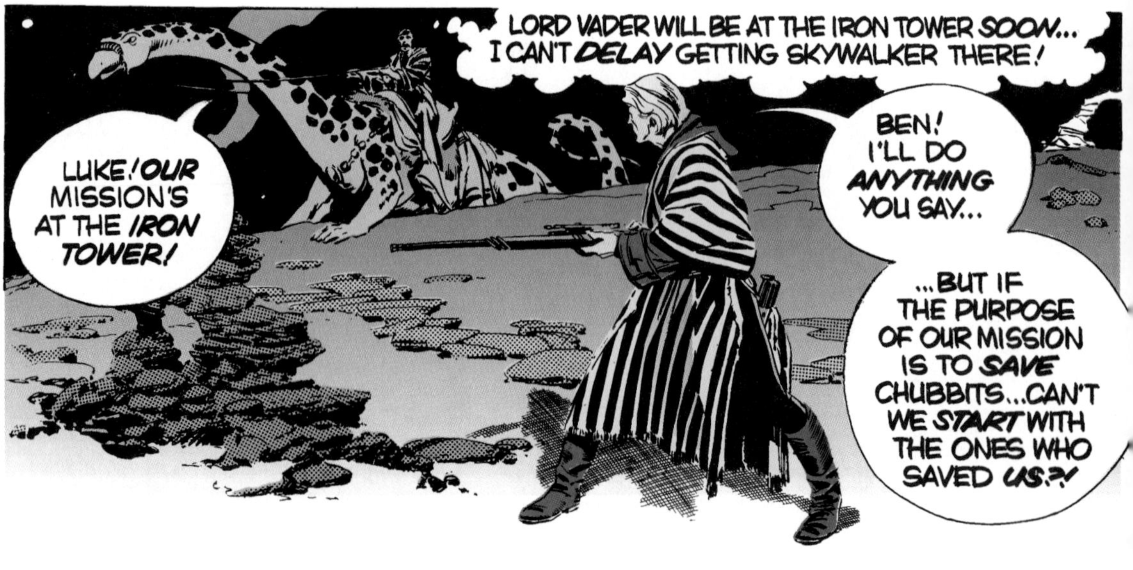
LORD VADER WILL BE AT THE IRON TOWER SOON... I CAN'T DELAY GETTING SKYWALKER THERE!
LUKE! OUR MISSION'S AT THE IRON TOWER!
BEN! I'LL DO ANYTHING YOU SAY...
...BUT IF THE PURPOSE OF OUR MISSION IS TO SAVE CHUBBITS...CAN'T WE START WITH THE ONES WHO SAVED US?!

WHAT WOULD THE *REAL* OBI-WAN KENOBI DO?

An Imperial shuttle craft swoops toward an ominous site...the *IRON TOWER!*

LORD VADER! SCANNERS SHOW *FIGHTING* NEARBY... TWO *HUMANS* HAVE JOINED ARIDUS LOCALS ATTACKING A PATROL SPEEDER!

WHAT?! THE ACTOR RISKS SKYWALKER'S LIFE WHEN HE'S NEARLY *MINE?!*

SHALL WE STEP INTO THE *SKIRMISH,* LORD VADER?

NO, COMMANDER. RETURN TO OUR CRUISER IN ORBIT.

TO BE *CONVINCING* IN HIS ROLE OF OBI-WAN KENOBI, OUR ACTOR MUST BE ALLOWED TO *IMPROVISE.* HE *KNOWS* I'LL PROVIDE *HARSH* CRITICISM...

"...SHOULD *ANYTHING* GO WRONG!'"

BEN! *BEN!*

LUKE! WHAT *IS* IT?!

LUKE, ARE YOU *ALL RIGHT?* WHEN I CAUSED THE BLAST BY TOUCHING MY LIGHTSABER TO THE PATROL SPEEDER'S *POWER CELLS,* I FEARED--

IT FINISHED THE *IMPERIALS,* NOT ME! I WAS AFRAID THE EXPLOSION GOT *YOU,* BEN!

MAYBE WE *SHOULDN'T* HAVE RISKED OUR MISSION DOING THIS...

...BUT YOU CAN'T SAY IT ISN'T *APPRECIATED!*

YET, IT'S ONLY *PROLONGED* THE MOMENT WHEN I *BETRAY* YOU!

Smoke curls over the ruin of the Imperial patrol speeder...

MAYBE WE *SHOULD* HAVE PUT OUR MISSION AHEAD OF JUMPING BACK INTO THE *FIGHT...* BUT THIS MAKES ME *REALLY GLAD* WE DIDN'T!

YES, LUKE... I-IT'S... MOST GRATIFYING...

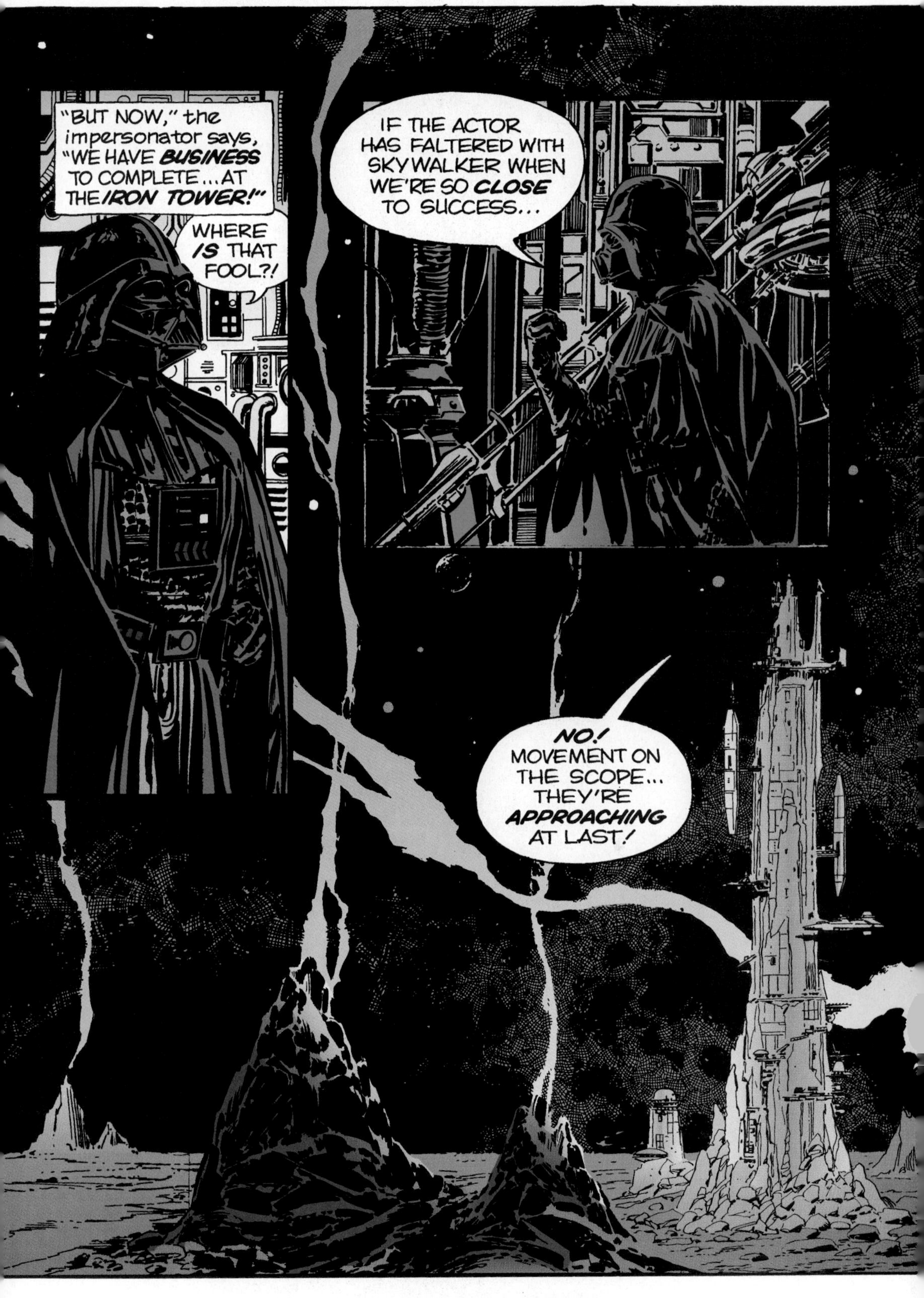
"BUT NOW," the impersonator says, "WE HAVE BUSINESS TO COMPLETE...AT THE IRON TOWER!"
WHERE IS THAT FOOL?!
IF THE ACTOR HAS FALTERED WITH SKYWALKER WHEN WE'RE SO CLOSE TO SUCCESS...
NO! MOVEMENT ON THE SCOPE... THEY'RE APPROACHING AT LAST!

PART 11

THOSE LITTLE CHUBBITS REALLY LOVE AND *ADMIRE* YOU, BEN...

SOMEDAY MAYBE *I* CAN WIN THE SAME KIND OF RESPECT...WITH *YOU* TO TEACH ME.

ER... SOMEDAY, LUKE, BUT FOR NOW...

...THE *IRON TOWER* WAITS!

TERRAIN'S CHANGING, BEN...MORE *OMINOUS!*

ARIDUS'S MINING REGION, LUKE...THE *LAVA PITS.* OUR *DESTINATION* IS JUST AHEAD.

WHATEVER THE OUTCOME... IT'S *GREAT* TO BE AT YOUR SIDE AGAIN. KNOWING DARTH VADER DIDN'T *REALLY* DESTROY YOU ON THE DEATH STAR...I CAN FACE *ANYTHING!*

And...

YOU'RE *NEAR,* SKYWALKER...SOON YOU'LL SENSE MY *PRESENCE!* ONLY YOU'LL MISTAKENLY BELIEVE IT'S THE *FORCE* RADIATING FROM YOUR OLD MENTOR...

...UNTIL *TOO LATE!*

THERE, LUKE...THE *IRON TOWER!*

YOU MUST HAVE USED THE *FORCE* GETTING THROUGH THE LAVA PITS SAFELY, BEN...I CAN *FEEL* IT.

"FROM HERE ON," says the impersonator, "THAT FEELING WILL **GROW.** WE'RE GOING **IN!"**

HURRY, ACTOR...THIS CONFRONTATION WITH SKYWALKER HAS BEEN **TOO LONG** COMING!

Inside the Iron Tower...

TIME TO **SEPARATE,** LUKE! THAT **HATCH** LEADS TO THE EMERGENCY STAIRS... TAKE THEM TO THE **CONTROL CHAMBER!**

I'LL TAKE CARE OF THESE **DEATHTRAP MECHANISMS...** YOU PROCEED DIRECTLY TO SABOTAGE THE MAIN CONTROLS! AND.. BE **CAREFUL,** YOUNGSTER!

I'M NOT **WORRIED...**

...NOT WHEN I'M WORKING WITH **YOU,** BEN!

Determinedly, Luke advances up the Iron Tower's emergency stairs...with automated **DEATH BEAMS** challenging every step! Then...

THEY'VE **STOPPED!** BEN SUCCEEDED IN **NULLIFYING** THEIR ENERGY SOURCE!

HE'S STILL USING THE **FORCE...**FEELS SO **STRONG...** ALMOST **TOO** STRONG...**DARK...**

And in the giant power generator's tower...

SKYWALKER'S *SUSPICION* IS RISING, ACTOR.! JOIN ME IN THE *CONTROL CHAMBER*...I REQUIRE A *FINAL SCENE* FROM YOU!

As Luke cautiously makes his way toward the Iron Tower's control chamber...

...a personnel lift carries the impersonator there *AHEAD* of him!

TIME TO ADD THE *CROWNING TOUCH* TO YOUR PERFORMANCE, ACTOR!

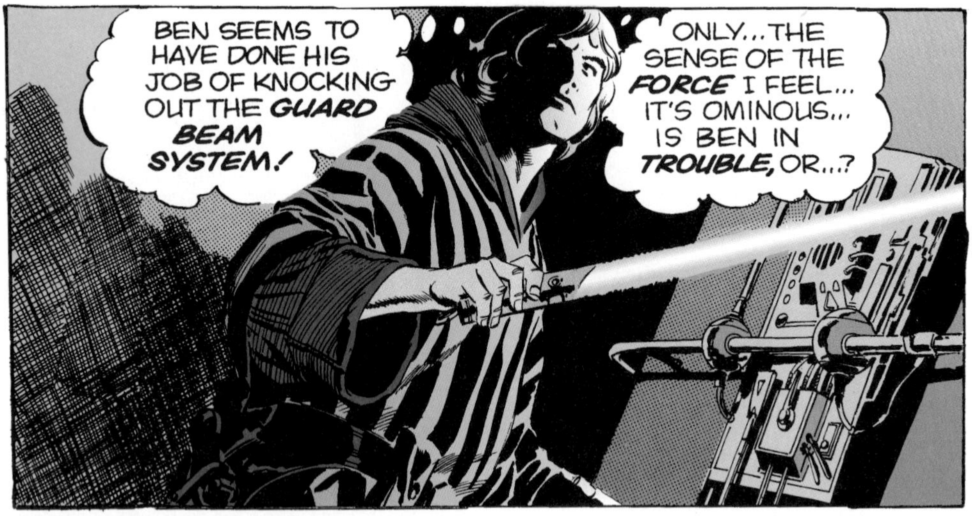
BEN SEEMS TO HAVE DONE HIS JOB OF KNOCKING OUT THE GUARD BEAM SYSTEM!
ONLY... THE SENSE OF THE FORCE I FEEL... IT'S OMINOUS... IS BEN IN TROUBLE, OR...?

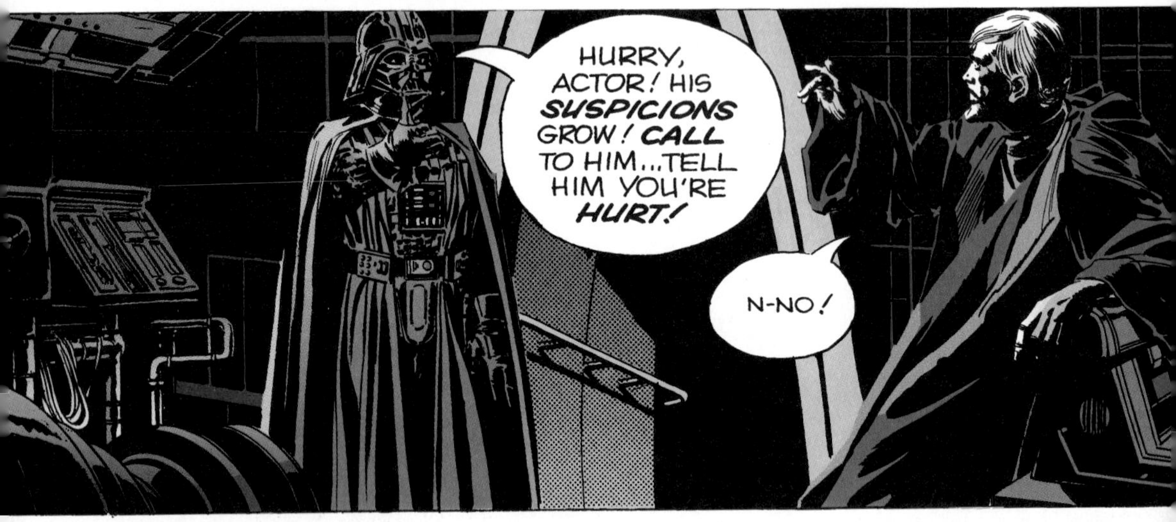
HURRY, ACTOR! HIS SUSPICIONS GROW! CALL TO HIM...TELL HIM YOU'RE HURT!
N-NO!

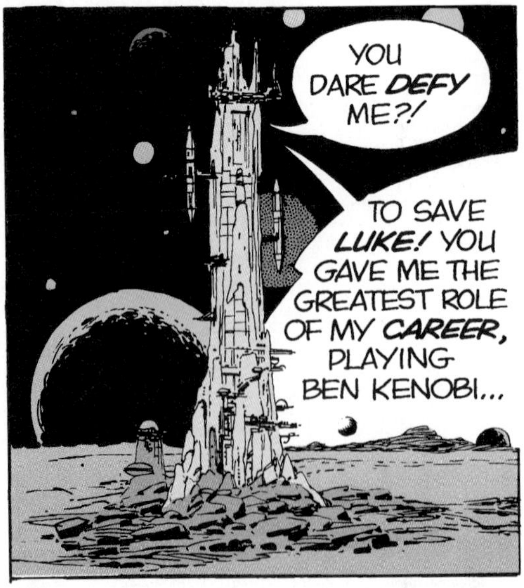
YOU DARE DEFY ME?!
TO SAVE LUKE! YOU GAVE ME THE GREATEST ROLE OF MY CAREER, PLAYING BEN KENOBI...

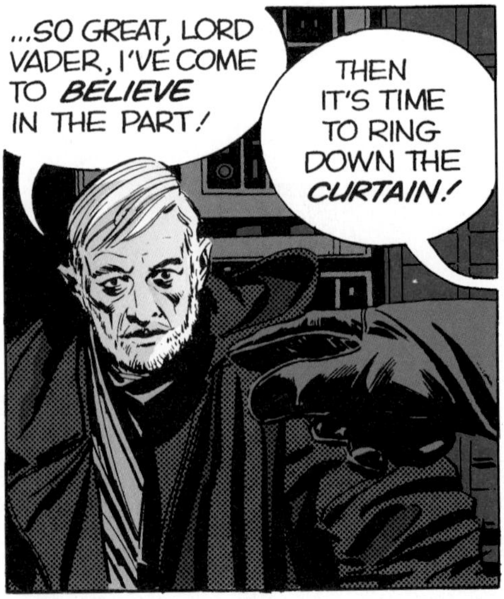
...SO GREAT, LORD VADER, I'VE COME TO BELIEVE IN THE PART!
THEN IT'S TIME TO RING DOWN THE CURTAIN!

A *GESTURE* from the Lord of the Sith...and the impersonator's defiance is instantly *PUNISHED!*

F-FINALLY...YOU'VE MADE A... *MISTAKE,* LORD VADER! YOUR METHOD...OF *DISPATCHING* ME...

"...IS *BOUND* TO BE FELT BY LUKE FOR WHAT IT *IS!*"

THE *DARK SIDE* OF THE FORCE! ONLY *ONE PERSON* COULD BE USING THAT!

SKYWALKER'S *ALERTED* TO MY TRAP... I'VE GOT TO GO *AFTER* HIM! ACTOR, PRAY *DEATH* TAKES YOU BEFORE I RETURN!

But as *DARTH VADER* moves...

...so does the fatally injured man who should be *INCAPABLE* of it...

...to a button on the *COMMUNICATOR*...and a *CONTROL SWITCH.*

POWER OVERLOAD! The suddenly strained circuitry of the Iron Tower gives way... *EXPLOSIVELY!*

A series of blasts that *seem CERTAIN* to catch...

...EVERYONE!

As destruction dies in the Iron Tower...

L-LUKE? I STARTED THE POWER OVERLOAD IN THE *UPPER LEVELS*...HOPING THE BLAST WOULDN'T REACH YOU.

YOU WERE *RIGHT!* I WOULDN'T *BE* HERE OTHERWISE, BEN!

S-SURELY YOU'VE REALIZED...I'M *NOT* YOUR OLD MENTOR... JUST AN IMPOSTER... WHO CAME...TO *LOVE* THE PART...

...ONLY HOPE I PLAYED IT... WELL...

From the distance, Luke's ship appears... summoned by the man who now grows silent. And still.

MASTER LUKE! WHAT'S *HAPPENED?!* AN *EMERGENCY DIRECTIONAL BEACON* FLASHED IN THE SHIP AND I CAME FAST AS I COULD!

THE IRON TOWER WAS A *TRAP* SET BY DARTH VADER...

...BUT THIS MAN CAUSED IT TO *BACKFIRE!* HE MUST'VE SIGNALED YOU JUST BEFORE HITTING THE TOWER'S *OVERLOAD CIRCUITS!*

THIS WAS AN *ACTOR* TRAINED TO *IMPERSONATE* BEN! ONLY, LIVING THE ROLE *CHANGED* HIM...

...WHEN THE CHIPS WERE DOWN, HE DID WHAT THE *REAL* BEN WOULD HAVE!

ONE THING, SIR... *LORD VADER* SEEMINGLY PERISHED IN THE EXPLOSION!

I *WONDER*, THREEPIO! SOMEHOW, I DOUBT WE'LL *EVER* BE FREE OF HIM SO EASILY!

Meanwhile, the Rebel Alliance high command looks upon the instrument which may *DESTROY* them!

IT'S *DARTH VADER'S* PRIVATE CRUISER...AND *NOTHING* WE HAVE CAN *STOP* IT!

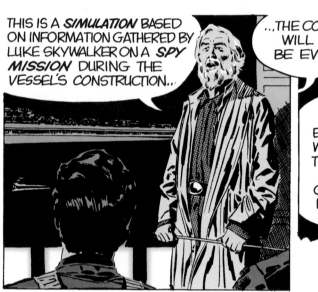

THIS IS A *SIMULATION* BASED ON INFORMATION GATHERED BY LUKE SKYWALKER ON A *SPY MISSION* DURING THE VESSEL'S CONSTRUCTION...

...THE COMPLETED CRAFT WILL UNDOUBTEDLY BE EVEN *STRONGER!*

WE FOUND AN EXPLOITABLE WEAKNESS IN THE *DEATH STAR*, GENERAL DODONNA...

...THERE MUST BE SOME *SIMILAR* SPOT IN DARTH VADER'S NEW CRUISER!

SEVERAL *POSSIBILITIES*, PRINCESS...IF WE COULD SACRIFICE A *FLEET* TO BREAK ITS *SHIELDING SYSTEM!*

GENERAL DODONNA, WE MAY SUCCESSFULLY *RELOCATE* OUR BASE *BEFORE* VADER'S NEW CRUISER IS READY!

WE MUST *PLAN* IN CASE WE *DON'T*, MY FRIENDS!

...AND TO *FIGHT* THE DARK LORD'S MONSTER SHIP, WE *FIRST* HAVE TO FIND A WAY TO *PENETRATE* ITS SHIELD SYSTEM.

POWER GEM...

WHAT WAS THAT, PRINCESS LEIA?

SOMETHING I ONCE HEARD MY *FATHER* MENTION ...WHEN I WAS A LITTLE GIRL... BACK IN THE DAYS OF THE OLD *REPUBLIC!*

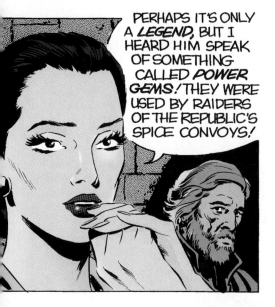

PERHAPS IT'S ONLY A *LEGEND,* BUT I HEARD HIM SPEAK OF SOMETHING CALLED *POWER GEMS!* THEY WERE USED BY RAIDERS OF THE REPUBLIC'S SPICE CONVOYS!

I REMEMBER NOW, YOUR HIGHNESS...IT'S NO *LEGEND!* THE SO-CALLED *POWER GEMS* WERE USED BY THE SPACE PIRATES OF *IRIDIUM!*

"THE *AURA* RADIATED BY THE JEWELS SOMEHOW *DISRUPTED* THE LARGER SHIPS' *MAGNETIC SHIELDS!*"

IF THEY CAN DISRUPT THE *FORCE SHIELDS*, GENERAL DODONNA... THEY'RE *EXACTLY* WHAT WE NEED AGAINST DARTH VADER'S NEW CRUISER!

EXCEPT JEDI KNIGHTS *SMASHED* THE PIRATE OPERATION...

...AND THE GEMS *PERISHED* WITH THE PIRATE SHIPS!

PERHAPS NOT *ALL*! IF WE KNEW SOMEONE THOROUGHLY *FAMILIAR* WITH THE GALAXY'S *OUTLAW* ELEMENT...

I'M AFRAID THE NOTION OF LOCATING A *POWER GEM* TO USE AGAINST DARTH VADER'S NEW DREADNAUGHT IS *FANCIFUL*, YOUR MAJESTY! EVEN IF ONE ACTUALLY STILL *EXISTS*...

...WHO KNOWS THE *INTERGALACTIC UNDERWORLD* WELL ENOUGH TO PROWL THERE AND *UNCOVER* IT?

Leia seeks out Han Solo...

WHAT?! CHEWIE AN' ME CHASE ALL OVER THE GALAXY FOR SOMETHING THAT PROBABLY DOESN'T *EXIST?!*

...EADERSHIP RESPONSIBILITIES RE AFFECTING YOUR *JUDGMENT,* 'RINCESS! YOU NEED A *DIVERSION*...OF AN *AFFECTIONATE* NATURE!

WE NEED AN *EDGE* AGAINST DARTH VADER'S *NEW SHIP*...

...IF *YOU'RE* TOO BUSY, MAYBE *LUKE* WILL HELP! HE'S RETURNING SOON!

HUH? THE KID DOESN'T HAVE THE *EXPERIENCE* THIS JOB NEEDS!

LUKE DOESN'T KNOW THE GALACTIC *UNDERWORLD*, LEIA... AND IF A POWER GEM EXISTS, *THAT'S* WHERE YOU'LL FIND IT!

DOES THIS MEAN YOU *VOLUNTEER?*

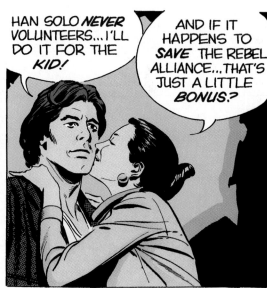

HAN SOLO *NEVER* VOLUNTEERS...I'LL DO IT FOR THE *KID!*

AND IF IT HAPPENS TO *SAVE* THE REBEL ALLIANCE...THAT'S JUST A LITTLE *BONUS.?*

DON'T *WORRY,* YOUR ROYALNESS... SOMEDAY I'M HITTING YOU PEOPLE WITH A *BILL* FOR *ALL* MY SERVICES!

From Rebel Headquarters on Yavin's fourth moon, the *MILLENNIUM FALCON* runs the Imperial Blockade...

...and leaps through *HYPERSPACE* to...

...*JUNKFORT STATION*, CHEWIE! LOTTA SHIPS GET ILLEGAL EQUIPMENT AND MODIFICATIONS HERE...

...I DOUBT THEY KEEP *POWER GEMS* IN STOCK, BUT IT'S SOMEWHERE TO *START!*

Han and Chewie bring the *FALCON* into one of the outworld space station's docking bays...

SOLO! DIDN'T EXPECT TO SEE *YOU* ON JUNKFORT...

...NOT SINCE *JABBA THE HUTT* PUT A *PRICE* ON YOUR HEAD!

I THOUGHT THEY KEPT *BOUNTY HUNTERS AWAY* FROM HERE!

ANYONE CAN BE TEMPTED AT JABBA'S PRICES. WATCH YOUR *BACK!*

WHILE WE'RE ASKING ABOUT *POWER GEMS* IN THE LOCAL CANTINA... WATCH *EVERYTHING*, CHEWIE

POWER GEMS? LIKE THE 'OL SPACE PIRATES OF *IRIDIUM* USED?!

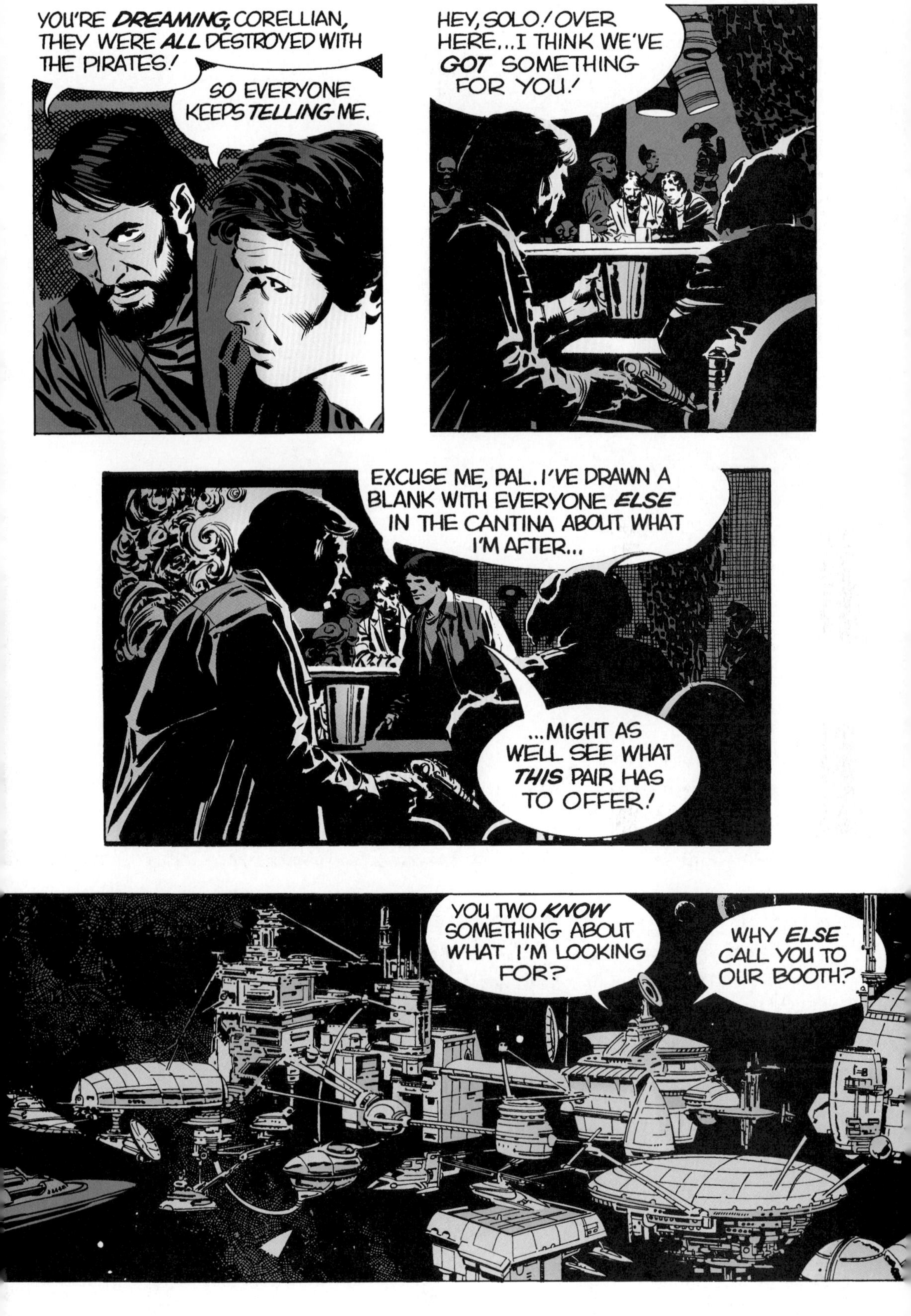

YOU'RE DREAMING, CORELLIAN, THEY WERE ALL DESTROYED WITH THE PIRATES!
SO EVERYONE KEEPS TELLING ME.
HEY, SOLO! OVER HERE...I THINK WE'VE GOT SOMETHING FOR YOU!
EXCUSE ME, PAL.. I'VE DRAWN A BLANK WITH EVERYONE ELSE IN THE CANTINA ABOUT WHAT I'M AFTER...
...MIGHT AS WELL SEE WHAT THIS PAIR HAS TO OFFER!
YOU TWO KNOW SOMETHING ABOUT WHAT I'M LOOKING FOR?
WHY ELSE CALL YOU TO OUR BOOTH?

WELL, WORD SEEMS TO BE OUT THAT JABBA THE HUTT PUT A *PRICE* ON MY HEAD...

NO *BOUNTY HUNTERS* ALLOWED HERE, SOLO!

THE OFFER COULD MAKE *ANYONE* GREEDY... MAYBE GREEDY ENOUGH TO THINK I DON'T *KNOW* THE BLASTER UNDER THE *TABLE* TRICK...

NOW *YOU'RE* GONNA LEARN THE CONSEQUENCES OF PICKING ON SOMEONE WITH A *WOOKIEE* PARTNER!

UH...JUST AS *SOON* AS HE *JOINS* US!

CHEWIE! CHEWBACCA! IF YOU CAN TEAR YOURSELF AWAY FROM THAT *CONVERSATION* A MOMENT...

...I NEED HELP!

VOROWRK!

As a finger tightens on the trigger of the blaster aimed at Han...

RAWWWK!

BWAAARK!

YEAH, YOU FIXED THOSE AMATEUR BOUNTY HUNTERS REAL *GOOD*, CHEWIE... ONCE YOU GOT *AROUND* TO IT!

WHAT WAS THAT LITTLE TWERP AT THE BAR SAYING THAT KEPT YOU TOO *SPELLBOUND* TO RUSH TO MY RESCUE?

NAARAWGH!

HE'D *HEARD* OF A PLACE WHERE THERE MIGHT BE A *POWER GEM*?!

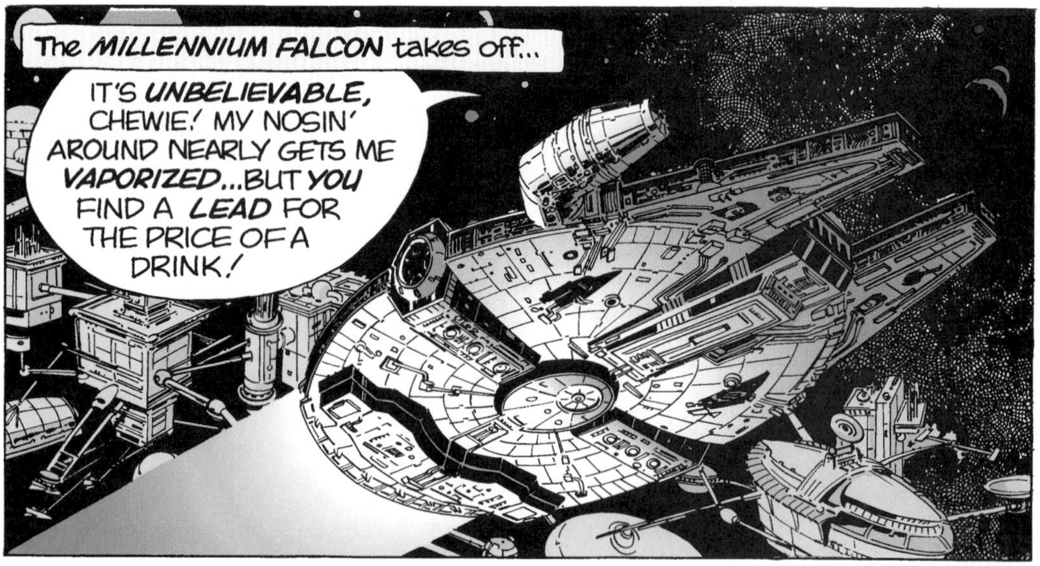
The MILLENNIUM FALCON takes off...
IT'S UNBELIEVABLE, CHEWIE! MY NOSIN' AROUND NEARLY GETS ME VAPORIZED...BUT YOU FIND A LEAD FOR THE PRICE OF A DRINK!

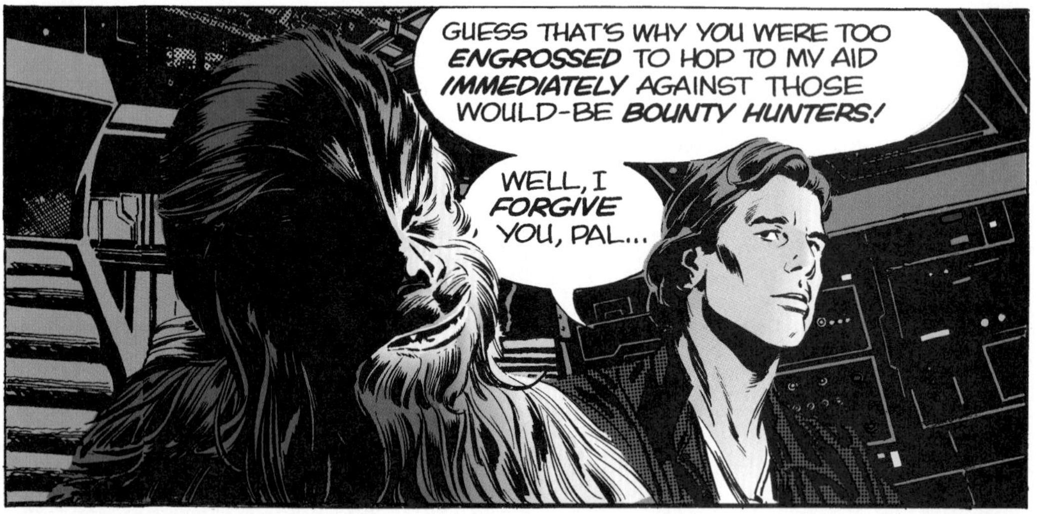
GUESS THAT'S WHY YOU WERE TOO ENGROSSED TO HOP TO MY AID IMMEDIATELY AGAINST THOSE WOULD-BE BOUNTY HUNTERS!
WELL, I FORGIVE YOU, PAL...

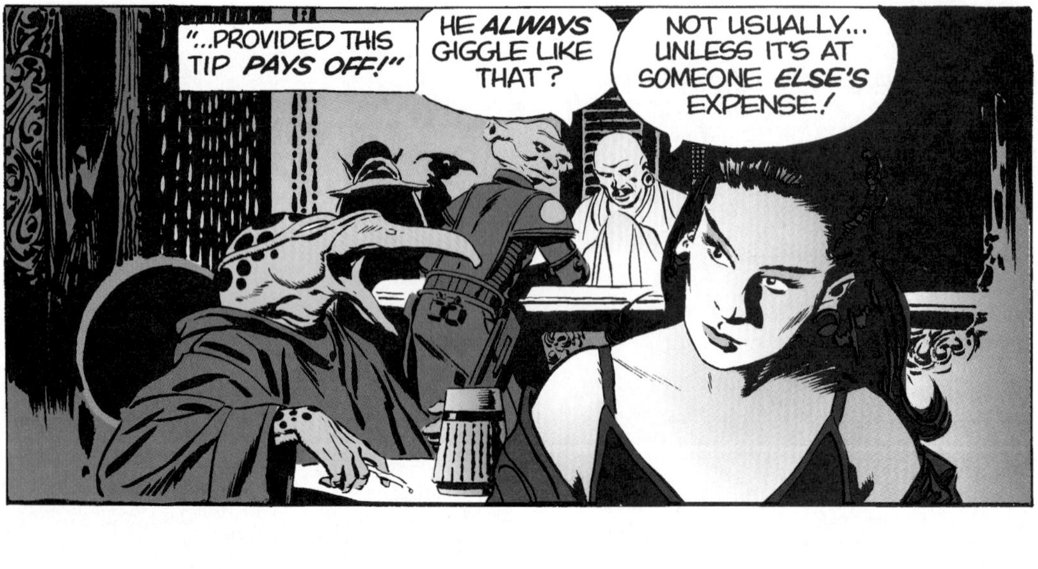
"...PROVIDED THIS TIP PAYS OFF!"
HE ALWAYS GIGGLE LIKE THAT?
NOT USUALLY... UNLESS IT'S AT SOMEONE ELSE'S EXPENSE!

HERE WE *ARE*, CHEWIE! DOESN'T LOOK LIKE MUCH... BUT IT'S FAR ENOUGH FROM *IMPERIAL* CIRCLES TO BE PROMISING!

LOOKS LIKE A JILLION OTHER PLACES WHERE WE'VE HID OUT OR DONE BUSINESS.

STRANGERS! MORE *COMPETITION!*

NOT THAT THESE BACKWATER PLANETS ARE *TOTALLY* WITHOUT ATTRACTION!

DON'T MAKE ANY *LONG-RANGE PLANS*, STAR-HOPPER.

YOU AND THE FUZZBALL DON'T LOOK LIKE *GAMBLERS* OR *TOURISTS*, CORELLIAN... ODDS ARE YOU'VE COME FOR THE *POWER GEM!*

WE FIGURE THERE'S ENOUGH *COMPETITION* ALREADY-- SO WE WAIT HERE AT THE LANDING FIELD TO *DISCOURAGE* ANY NEW PROSPECTS!

YOU'RE TALKIN' FLEE OR FIGHT? LET'S *DISCUSS* THIS A LITTLE, GUYS!

As Han speaks, he also slowly *MOVES*...

ENOUGH, CORELLIAN! IF YOU AND THE WOOKIEE AREN'T READY TO LEAVE...GET READY TO *FIGHT!*

OKAY, CHUCKLES, *YOU* CALLED IT! BUT--

STOP NOW! THE ONLY COMBAT TOLERATED *HERE* IS THE *OFFICIAL ONE* FOR THE POWER GEM!

YOU THREE WERE TRYING TO ELIMINATE *COMPETITION!* GET OFF THE PLANET... *FAST!*

WE *PAID* FOR A CHANCE AT THE *POWER GEM!*

YOU WOULDN'T HAVE SURVIVED *THIS!* THE CORELLIAN MANEUVERED SO THE *SUN* WAS IN YOUR EYES,...AND HE AND THE WOOKIEE HAVE YOU IN A *CROSSFIRE!*

NICE TO MEET A LADY WHO KNOWS HER *BUSINESS,* HUH, CHEWIE?

THEN YOU WON'T RESIST DOING *EXACTLY* AS I ORDER, HAN SOLO!

ONTO THE *FLOATER!* BOTH YOU *AND* THE WOOKIEE!

YOU *KNOW* ME, LADY?

THE NAME IS *MYSTRA!* OUR AGENT ON *JUNKFORT STATION* SENT WORD ABOUT YOU.

THAT WOULD BE YOUR LITTLE *DRINKING BUDDY,* CHEWIE...

...WHAT KIND OF *MESS* HAS HE STEERED US INTO?

ONE THAT *COULD* GET YOU WHAT YOU SEEK...THE *POWER GEM!*

Han and Chewbacca are taken toward the rimworld planet's lone city...

UH... WHERE EXACTLY ARE WE *HEADED*, MYSTRA?

YOU'RE HERE FOR THE *POWER GEM*, CAPTAIN SOLO...

...DON'T YOU WANT TO MEET THE MAN WHO'S GIVING IT *AWAY?*

FROM THE HOSTILE GREETING CHEWIE AN' I GOT AT THE LANDING FIELD...I GATHER THERE'S A LITTLE *COMPETITION* FOR YOUR FRIEND'S GENEROSITY.

MYSTRA! THAT'S AN *ARENA* DOWN THERE!

EXACTLY, CAPTAIN SOLO!

WHAT?!

ROWWL-GRRFFF?!

ANYONE WHO WANTS THE *POWER GEM* MUST *FIGHT* FOR IT...AND *PAY* FOR THE RIGHT TO *DO* SO!

MYSTRA, YOU'VE GOT JOKERS *PAYING* FOR THE CHANCE TO GET THEIR *HEADS* BUSTED IN THAT ARENA?

THE GALAXY'S *FULL* OF OVER-CONFIDENT SCOUNDRELS...

...THEY ALL *EXPECT* TO WIN, SOLO! AND THE *ULTIMATE* WINNER GETS THE *POWER GEM!*

MEANTIME, SOMEONE *ELSE* GETS VERY *RICH* OFF THE *LOSERS!*

YES. THE MAN YOU'RE ABOUT TO *MEET!*

Mystra's floater lands inside the city's largest villa...

AH... THE FAMOUS CAPTAIN AND FIRST MATE OF THE *MILLENNIUM FALCON!* WELCOME! YOUR REPUTATIONS *PRECEDE* YOU...

...*PARTICULARLY* THE PART ABOUT THAT LARGE *BOUNTY* JABBA THE HUTT IS OFFERING!

I'M *RASKAR!* FORMER SPACE PIRATE...AND *OWNER* OF THE LAST SURVIVING *POWER GEM!*

RASKAR, IF YOU BROUGHT CHEWIE AN' ME HERE FIGURING TO COLLECT ON THE HUTT'S *REWARD*...

...YOU'LL NEED MORE THAN THAT OVER-SIZED *KITCHEN UTENSIL* TO MAKE IT STICK!

YOU *MISJUDGE* ME, SOLO! I'VE LONG *ABANDONED* SPACE-PIRATE STYLE VIOLENCE...

...MY SWORDPLAY'S STRICTLY FOR *EXERCISE!* THESE DAYS, *MYSTRA* DOES ALL MY KILLING!

HA! I WIN AGAIN! THIS PRACTICE DROID'S PROGRAMMING WILL HAVE TO BE *UPGRADED!*

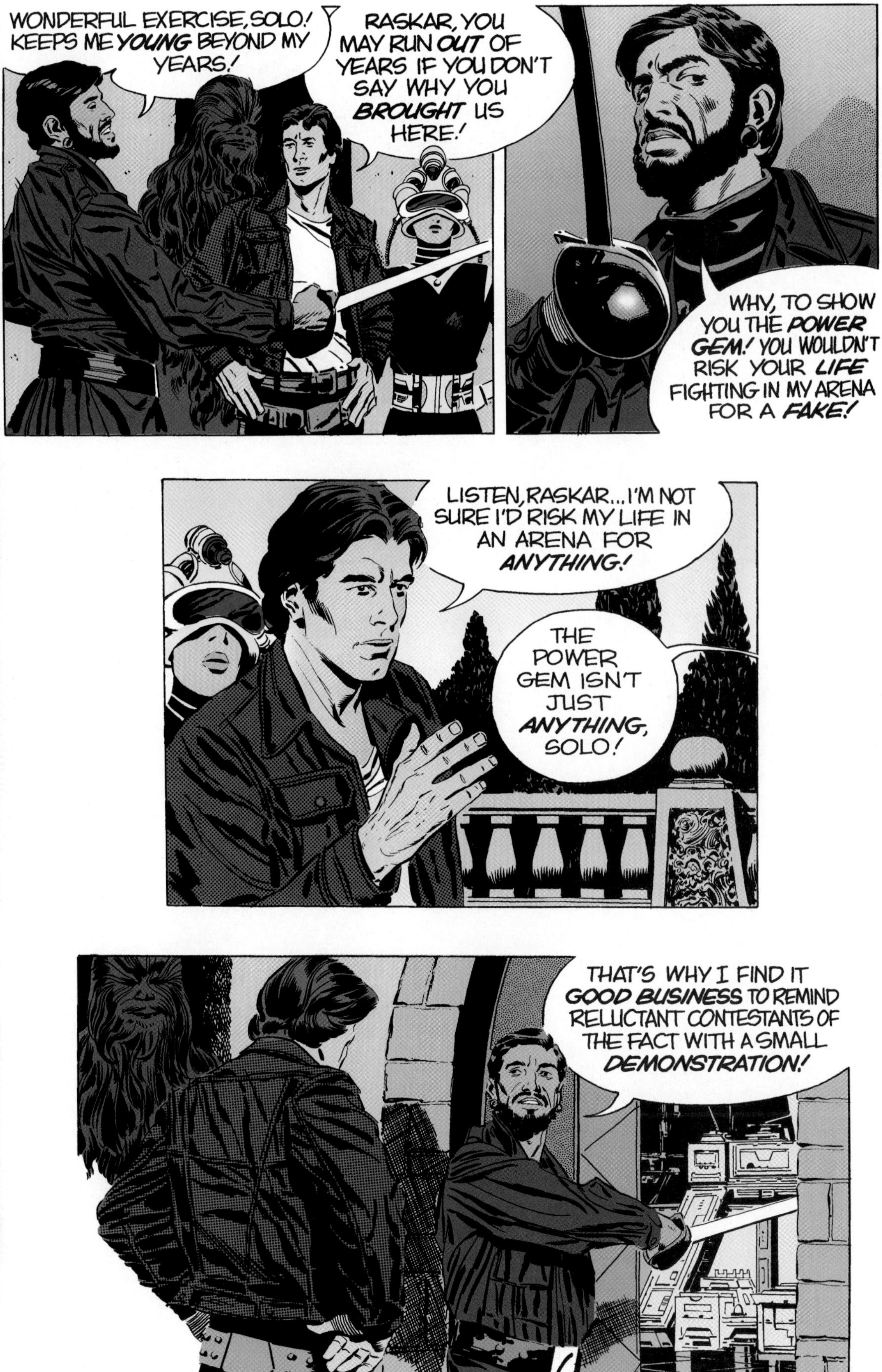

WONDERFUL EXERCISE, SOLO! KEEPS ME YOUNG BEYOND MY YEARS!
RASKAR, YOU MAY RUN OUT OF YEARS IF YOU DON'T SAY WHY YOU BROUGHT US HERE!
WHY, TO SHOW YOU THE POWER GEM! YOU WOULDN'T RISK YOUR LIFE FIGHTING IN MY ARENA FOR A FAKE!
LISTEN, RASKAR... I'M NOT SURE I'D RISK MY LIFE IN AN ARENA FOR ANYTHING!
THE POWER GEM ISN'T JUST ANYTHING, SOLO!
THAT'S WHY I FIND IT GOOD BUSINESS TO REMIND RELUCTANT CONTESTANTS OF THE FACT WITH A SMALL DEMONSTRATION!

THE LAST REMAINING *POWER GEM,* SOLO! MY DEAR...

...OPEN FIRE ON IT!

HEY! NO!

But...

THE BLAST ISN'T *TOUCHING* IT....!

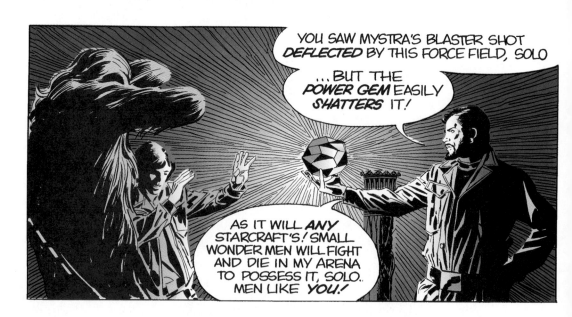

YOU SAW MYSTRA'S BLASTER SHOT *DEFLECTED* BY THIS FORCE FIELD, SOLO

...BUT THE *POWER GEM* EASILY *SHATTERS* IT!

AS IT WILL *ANY* STARCRAFT'S! SMALL WONDER MEN WILL FIGHT AND DIE IN MY ARENA TO POSSESS IT, SOLO.. MEN LIKE *YOU!*

OKAY. I'M IMPRESSED. ONLY, IF IT'S *THIS* GOOD...

...HOW COME YOU'RE SO WILLING TO *PART* WITH IT?!

A GEM WITH AN AURA THAT SHATTERS *FORCE FIELDS* CAN BE PUT TO A *LOT* OF USES, RASKAR! MOST OF 'EM *PROFITABLE* IF NOT PARTICU-LARLY *LEGAL!*

I'M ONE OF THE *ORIGINAL* SPACE PIRATES OF IRIDIUM, SOLO...

THE JEDI KNIGHTS SUPPOSEDLY *DESTROYED* THEM ALL!

I WASN'T *ON* THAT LAST, FATAL RAID. SO I ESCAPED...AND LEARNED A *GREAT LESSON!*

USING THE POWER GEM, A GOOD SPACE PIRATE COULD REAP A *FORTUNE,* SOLO... BUT NOT FOR *LONG!*

ITS USE ATTRACTS *ATTENTION!* IT BROUGHT THE *JEDI KNIGHTS* ON MY OLD COMRADES...

...IT WOULD BRING THE *EMPIRE* TODAY!

MAYBE, RASKAR... AND MAYBE *NOT!*

AH! *THAT'S* THE ATTITUDE! IT KEEPS *CONTESTANTS* IN MY ARENA...AND *ME* IN MODEST WEALTH!

LOOK AT THEM, SOLO! THEY'VE EACH *PAID* FOR THE PRIVILEGE TO CONTEST FOR THE POWER GEM!

NO DOUBT YOU CHARGE THE ARENA AUDIENCE *ADMISSION* TOO!

CERTAINLY! AND I, OF COURSE, TAKE A PERCENTAGE OF ALL *GAMBLING* ON THE MATCHES!

RASKAR, YOU MAY HAVE RETIRED FROM THE BUSINESS...

...BUT YOU'RE *STILL* A PIRATE!

AND *YOUR* PARTICIPATION WILL OPEN ONE *MORE* MONETARY VISTA FOR ME!

DON'T GET YOUR HOPES UP. BADLY AS CHEWIE AN' I WANT THE *POWER GEM*...WE COULDN'T SCRAPE TOGETHER THAT *ENTRY FEE* YOU DEMAND!

SOLO, I'LL GLADLY LET YOU FIGHT IN MY ARENA FOR *NOTHING!*

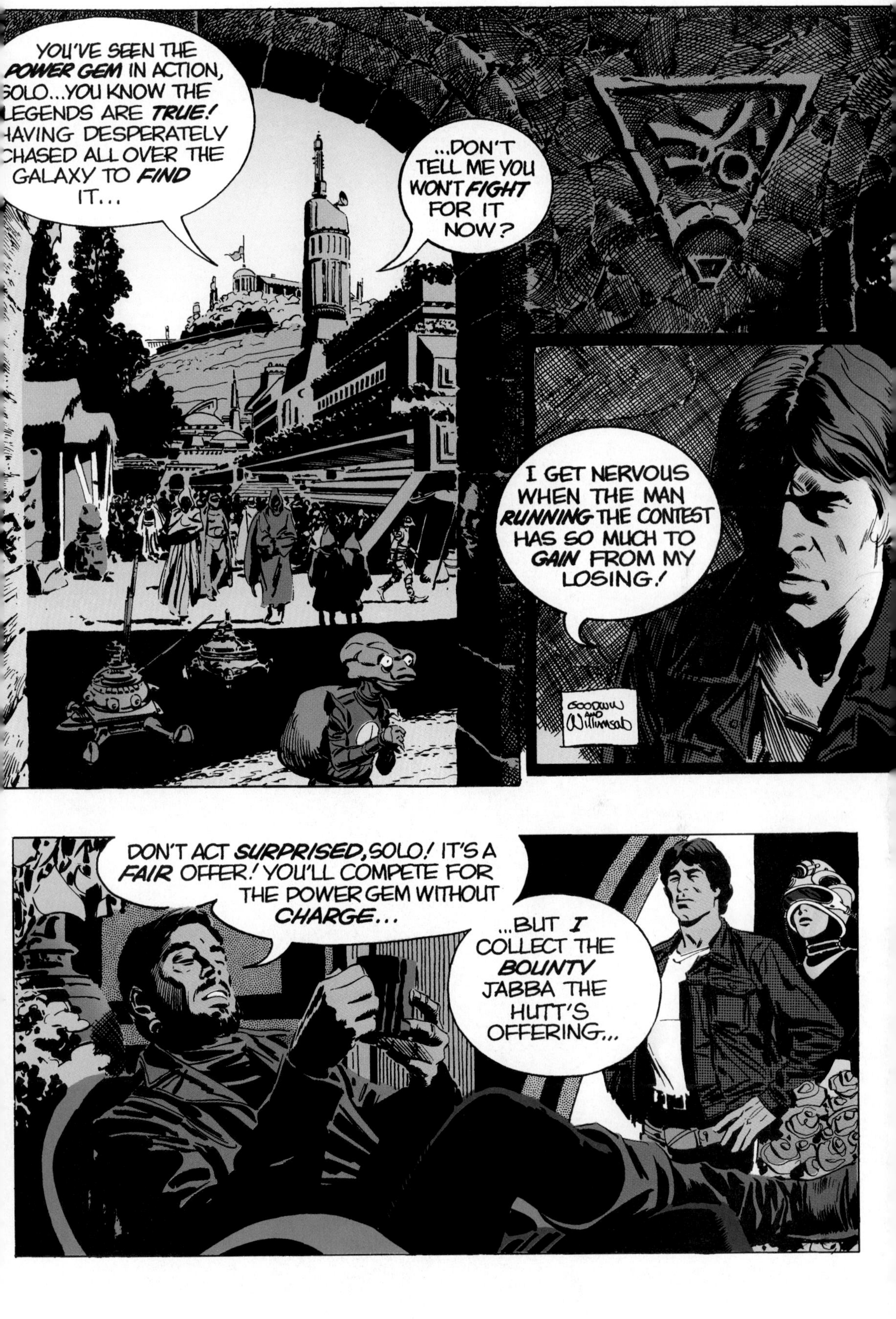
YOU'VE SEEN THE POWER GEM IN ACTION, SOLO...YOU KNOW THE LEGENDS ARE TRUE! HAVING DESPERATELY CHASED ALL OVER THE GALAXY TO FIND IT...
...DON'T TELL ME YOU WON'T FIGHT FOR IT NOW?
I GET NERVOUS WHEN THE MAN RUNNING THE CONTEST HAS SO MUCH TO GAIN FROM MY LOSING!
GOODWIN AND Williamson
DON'T ACT SURPRISED, SOLO! IT'S A FAIR OFFER! YOU'LL COMPETE FOR THE POWER GEM WITHOUT CHARGE...
...BUT I COLLECT THE BOUNTY JABBA THE HUTT'S OFFERING...

...AND CONSIDERING THE SIZE AND STRENGTH OF THE OTHER CONTESTANTS, I'VE AN *EXCELLENT* CHANCE OF COLLECTING!

ROW-AARK?!

TOO EXCELLENT, SPACE PIRATE...

...IT'S ONLY A DEAL IF *CHEWBACCA* FIGHTS IN MY PLACE!

I WANT *SOME* CHANCE OF *WINNING* THE POWER GEM IN YOUR ARENA!

AH! BUT IF THE WOOKIEE *LOSES*?

YOU *STILL* COLLECT THE *BOUNTY* JABBA THE HUTT PLACED ON MY *HIDE*!

AND I HAVE *MYSTRA*...TO SEE YOU DON'T VANISH *BEFORE* I COLLECT!

Business concluded...Han and his first mate depart Raskar's villa.

NAWROWWR!

YOU'RE *UPSET* THAT I VOLUNTEERED YOU TO FIGHT IN THE ARENA?

TRUST ME CHEWIE...I *KNOW* WHAT I'M DOIN'! HAVE I *EVER* LET YOU DOWN?

WROWAARK!

WELL... *BESIDES* THAT TIME!

PART 12

HALT RIGHT *THERE*, SOLO! YOU'RE FINISHED WITH RASKAR...BUT NOT *ME*!

DRAW, SOLO! *FAST!* YOUR *LIFE* DEPENDS ON IT!

THIS IS *CRAZY*, LADY! BUT IF IT'S WHAT YOU WANT--

OW! MYSTRA! W-WHAT?

BE GRATEFUL MY WEAPON WAS SET AT *STING LEVEL*, CORELLIAN! I WANTED TO *PROVE* SOMETHING.

YOU'RE NO *MATCH* FOR ME! *NO ONE* IS! WITH MY *CYBER-VISION*, I NEVER MISS...

...AND WITH THIS *WRIST-BLASTER*, I'M NEVER OUTDRAWN!

YOU'RE A *SCHEMER*, HAN SOLO! BUT IF YOUR PLANS TO GET OUR *POWER GEM* INVOLVE GOING AROUND *ME*...

...*FORGET* THEM... AND *LIVE* LONGER!

MYSTRA MAKES A GOOD CASE FOR PLAYING BY THE *RULES* TO WIN THE POWER GEM, CHEWIE!

GNRRAAGH!

EASY FOR ME TO SAY SINCE *I* WON'T BE THE ONE IN RASKAR'S ARENA...

PAL, IF THINGS GO ACCORDING TO PLAN...

...I PROMISE *YOU'LL* NEVER SET FOOT IN THERE, EITHER! *C'MON*...LET'S ARRANGE YOUR FIRST FIGHT!

?

RASKAR, THIS IS *MYSTRA*. I DELIVERED A LITTLE *WARNING* TO HAN SOLO TO KEEP HIM IN LINE...

...BUT MY GUESS IS HE'S ABOUT TO *IGNORE* IT!

ACCORDING TO THE *DIRECTIONS* I GOT...THIS IS WHERE THE LEADING *CONTENDER* FOR THE *POWER GEM* TRAINS!

VROWWF!

THAT'S RIGHT! DESPITE *VOLUNTEERING* YOU, I PROMISED YOU'D NEVER SET *FOOT* IN RASKAR'S *ARENA*...

AH! THERE'S OUR MAN! *GET* 'IM, CHEWIE... EVERYTHING DEPENDS ON YOUR CLOBBERING HIM *RIGHT HERE!*

VROWK-RR-VRGH.?

IF YOU DON'T FIGHT THIS BRUISER RIGHT *NOW...*

...YOU'LL BE MAKING A *LIAR* OF ME!

TRUST ME, CHEWIE! MY PLAN DEPENDS ON YOU BATTLING THIS HULK *RIGHT HERE* INSTEAD OF IN THE *ARENA* AS RASKAR EXPECTS!

POW!

UH..., MY PLAN *ALSO* DEPENDS ON THE FIGHT LASTING AS *LONG* AS POSSIBLE!

NARROWWL!

At Han's urging, Chewbacca leaps up from where he's been hit!

RASKAR! THAT SHIFTY *CORELLIAN* AND HIS *WOOKIEE* FRIEND HAVE STARTED A *BRAWL*... WITH THE LEADING *CONTENDER* FOR THE POWER GEM!

BREAK IT *UP*, MYSTRA... *IMMEDIATELY!*

Mystra swiftly moves to stop Chewbacca's *BATTLE*, but...

IT'S *TOO LATE*, RASKAR! A *CROWD* HAS FORMED! *EVERYONE* IS TURNING OUT FOR THIS...

...WE'LL FACE A *RIOT* IF WE INTERFERE OR *HARM* EITHER FIGHTER!

MEANTIME, WE LOSE A *FORTUNE* BY NOT COLLECTING ARENA ADMISSIONS OR GAMBLING PERCENTAGES!

FIND *HAN SOLO!* I'LL HELP YOU SEARCH! THIS IS *HIS* DOING! WHATEVER HE'S UP TO, MYSTRA... HE'LL *PAY* FOR IT!

As Chewbacca keeps up his impromptu gladiatorial combat...

...Raskar rushes to join Mystra searching for Han Solo!

WON'T TAKE *LONG* TO FIND I'M NOT IN THE *CROWD* WATCHING THE FIGHT...

...BUT I DON'T *NEED* LONG TO REACH THE *POWER GEM!*

MY VILLA *ALARM SYSTEM* INDICATES THE POWER GEM CHAMBER IS BEING *FORCED OPEN,* MYSTRA!

OUR BOLD CORELLIAN IS DUE FOR A *FATAL* SURPRISE!

Stealthily, Han moves through Raskar's villa...

AH! OUR SPACE PIRATE'S ANTIQUE *PLAYTHING*... GIVES ME AN IDEA FOR THE *WORK* AT HAND.

BUT FIRST...LET'S SEE IF I'VE RETAINED ALL MY OLD LOCK SHORT-CIRCUITING SKILLS!

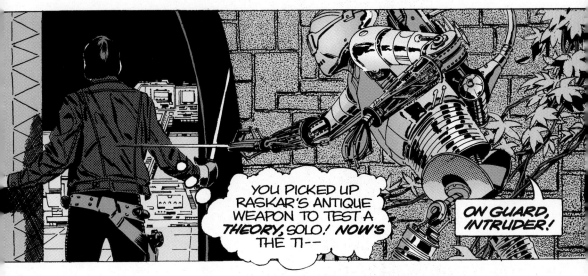

YOU PICKED UP RASKAR'S ANTIQUE WEAPON TO TEST A *THEORY*, SOLO! *NOW'S* THE TI--

ON GUARD, INTRUDER!

WHY DID YOU PICK UP MY MASTER'S *SWORD*, INTRUDER? DIDN'T YOU KNOW IT WOULD *ACTIVATE* ME?!

I *SUSPECTED*, TIN SOLDIER!

YOU SHOULD *ALSO* HAVE SUSPECTED I'M PROGRAMMED TO *KILL* THOSE NOT COMPETENT ENOUGH TO *OUTFIGHT* ME!

Disarmed, Han backs into the power gem chamber! But...

DIE, INTRUDER!

And as Raskar and Mystra approach the villa...

YOU'RE SLOWING DOWN! IF WE DON'T *RUSH*, SOLO MIGHT STILL--

HAN SOLO IS *DEAD!*

DEAD?!

MY FLOATER'S *ALARM DISPLAY* JUST REVEALED IT... HE'S TRIGGERED HIDDEN *DESTRUCT BEAMS* WHICH PROTECT THE POWER GEM!

PITY! HE POSSESSED QUALITIES I *ADMIRE*, MYSTRA! GREED... GUILE...

BUT THIS *SIMPLIFIES* YOUR COLLECTING THE *BOUNTY* ON HIM!

Meantime, unaware of the events at Raskar's villa...

...CHEWBACCA fights on!

Chewie seems to *TIRE!* The crowd senses a *KILL...*

While...

SOLO *DID* HAVE A CERTAIN CHARM...

IT NEVER QUITE EQUALLED JABBA THE HUTT'S *BOUNTY,* MYSTRA! HOPEFULLY, THE *DESTRUCT BEAMS* LEFT ENOUGH TO IDENTIFY AND--

SOLO! YOU SHOULD BE *DEAD!* THE HIDDEN *DESTRUCT BEAMS* WHICH PROTECT THE POWER GEM--

GOT YOUR *DUELING DROID* INSTEAD, RASKAR! YOU *OVER-PROGRAMMED* IT! THE THING WAS SO EAGER TO *SKEWER* ME...

...I *DODGED* AND LET *IT* LUNGE IN, ACTIVATING WHATEVER *DEFENSE MECHANISMS* YOU HAD PLANTED!

THEN I COULD SAFELY GET *CLOSE* TO THE POWER GEM ...WITH MY *POCKET SCANNER!*

THE GEM'S LOSING *POWER!* IT'S GOT ENOUGH FOR THOSE LITTLE *DEMONSTRATIONS* YOU STAGE...IT MIGHT EVEN SHATTER A BIG STARSHIP'S FORCE FIELD *ONCE* MORE.

BUT ONE-TIME USE ISN'T EXACTLY THE *PRIZE* ALL MY CONTESTANTS BELIEVE THEY'RE *FIGHTING* FOR!

AND *PAYING* TO DO SO! EVERYONE WILL BE VERY *MIFFED* AT THAT.

AH! BUT *WHO* WILL TELL THEM! MYSTRA... *KILL* OUR CLEVER FRIEND!

BIG *MISTAKE* RASKAR...I'M YOUR ONLY *HOP*

WHAT?! YOU USED YOUR POCKET SCANNER ON THE GEM... YOU *KNOW* IT ONLY HAS POWER ENOUGH TO BE USED *ONCE* MORE!

UNLIKE THE *OTHER* INTERGALACTIC SCOUNDRELS DECEIVED INTO FIGHTING FOR THIS BAUBLE..., ONCE IS ALL I *NEED!*

BESIDES...BLASTING *ME* COULD DESTROY THE *GEM!*

THAT JEWEL ISN'T BIG ENOUGH TO *HIDE* BEHIND, SOLO... NOT WITH THE *PRECISION FIRING* MY CYBER-VISION ALLOWS ME!

I CAN STILL *DROP* IT, LADY...

...AND CHIPPING OR SHATTERING THIS BABY COULD CAUSE ITS POWER TO DETERIORATE *FASTER!*

LOWER YOUR *WRIST-BLASTER*, MYSTRA...

...THE CAPTAIN SEEMS TO HAVE THOUGHT OF *EVERYTHING!*

PERHAPS EVEN HOW TO EMERGE FROM THIS WITH SOME *PROFIT*-- AND HOPEFULLY EVEN OUR *SKINS*-- INTACT!

RASKAR, YOU'VE MILKED THE GLADIATORIAL CONTEST FOR THE POWER GEM ALL YOU *CAN*... TIME TO DECLARE A *WINNER!*

YOU'RE *MAD*, SOLO!

...EVERYONE WHO PAID TO FIGHT WILL TEAR US LIMB FROM LIMB WHEN THE WINNER DISCOVERS THE GEM IS *LOSING* ITS POWER!

ONE WINNER WON'T *REVEAL* THAT...

...MY PAL, *CHEWBACCA!*

IF *THAT'S* YOUR PLAN...WE'RE *DOOMED!* CHECK OUR *FIGHT MONITORS*...THE WOOKIEE'S GOING DOWN IN *DEFEAT!*

THE BATTLEGROUND! Chewbacca falls once more! The watchful crowd tenses for the FINISH! Then...

GET UP, BIG BUDDY! YOU DON'T HAVE TO STRETCH THE FIGHT ANYMORE!

SOLO, IT'S TOO LATE! LOOK HOW TIRED YOUR WOOKIEE FRIEND IS!

I CAN SEE, MYSTRA...IT'S JUST WHAT I FEARED!

The killing blow descends... and is suddenly, mightily MET!

A BATTLE ENDS! And the crowd learns that a *TIRED* Wookiee is not a *DEFEATED* Wookiee...

...merely a very, very *ANGRY* one! There are no more challengers for the *POWER GEM!*

SOLO! *THAT'S* WHAT YOU FEARED?! I THOUGHT--

CHEWBACCA'S *TIRED* MYSTRA...THAT MAKES A WOOKIEE *VICIOUS!* GONNA BE *TOUGH* KEEPIN' HIM FROM *DESTROYIN'* THAT GUY!

SET THE FLOATER *DOWN* MYSTRA...! THIS WRAPS UP THE PROBLEM WITH THE *POWER GEM* AS WELL AS THE *FIGHT.*

...WE'LL BE ON OUR WAY ONCE I CAN SAFELY GET *CLOSE ENOUGH* TO LET CHEWIE KNOW HE'S ALREADY *WON!*

As the victors prepare to depart with their prize...

THERE, RASKAR! ISN'T THIS BETTER THAN *SHOOTING* ME?

BUT THE GEM WILL ONLY BE EFFECTIVE *ONE* MORE TIME, SOLO!

THAT STILL *HELPS* THE REBEL ALLIANCE... UNLIKE THE LARCENOUS TYPES COMPETING HERE...WHO COUNTED ON USING ITS FORCE SHIELD-DISRUPTING QUALITIES *OVER* AND *OVER!*

NOW OUR LITTLE DECEPTION WILL NEVER BE *SUSPECTED...* THANKS TO CHEWBACCA AND YOU!

WHAT A *WASTE,* EH, MYSTRA? A FINE SCOUNDREL SERVING SUCH A *RESPECTABLE* CAUSE!

RASKAR DOESN'T REALIZE THIS IS ONLY *TEMPORARY,* CHEWIE! SOMEDAY WE'LL *SHOW* 'IM...

...AN' RETURN TO FLEECE THAT PIRATE OUT OF *ALL* HIS ILL-GOTTEN GAINS!

The *MILLENNIUM FALCON* returns to Rebel Headquarters.

HAN! OH, *HAN!*

LUKE NEVER MADE IT BACK FROM HIS LAST MISSION!

LEIA, WHEN CHEWIE AN' I LEFT TO SEARCH FOR THE *POWER GEM*... YOU SAID LUKE WAS ON HIS WAY *BACK!*

HE *WAS*...

...BUT THE IMPERIALS HAVE *TIGHTENED* THEIR BLOCKADE ON OUR SECTOR OF SPACE! LUKE'S LAST REPORT INDICATED HE WAS HAVING *TROUBLE*...

"...WE HAVEN'T HEARD *ANYTHING* SINCE!"

HANG *ON,* THREEPIO... THEY'VE *FOUND* US AGAIN!

HOW ARE THOSE REPAIRS TO OUR *COMMUNICATOR* COMING, THREEPIO?

BLAST DAMAGE IS *ARTOO-DETOO'S* SPECIALTY, MASTER LUKE! BUT THOUGH HE ISN'T WITH US, REST ASSURED-- OH, DEAR! WE MAY HAVE TO *FORGET* CALLING FOR *HELP*, SIR!

WELL, THOSE *TIE FIGHTERS* AREN'T FORGETTING *US!* IF THE SCOPE DOESN'T TURN UP A *HIDING PLACE*, WE'RE... WE'RE...

SIR, WHAT *IS* IT?!

A *COMET!* THOSE INSIDIOUS IMPERIALS HAVE BEEN DRIVING US *INTO* ITS PATH! MASTER LUKE...WE'LL BE *DESTROYED!*

MAYBE *NOT*, THREEPIO!

SIR! WHAT ARE YOU *DOING?!* TURN *AWAY!* YOU'RE GUIDING US STRAIGHT *TOWARD* IT!

THAT SUSPECTED REBEL WE WERE PURSUING JUST *VANISHED* FROM THE SCOPES!

INSTEAD OF *TURNING*... THE NERVOUS FOOL *HIT* THE *COMET* WE PUSHED HIM TOWARD!

But... MASTER LUKE! WE'RE BEING CARRIED AWAY FROM OUR IMPERIAL PURSUERS *FASTER* THAN ANY *STARSHIP* COULD!

THAT'S THE *GOOD* PART, THREEPIO.

I HAD TO CUT IT *CLOSE*... SO WE'D BE PULLED INTO THIS FAST-FLYIN' MASS'S *SLIPSTREAM!*

ONLY PROBLEM IS... NOW *WE'RE* STUCK GOIN' WHEREVER *IT* DOES!

...THE *BAD* PART IS WE'RE *CAUGHT* IN THIS COMET'S SLIPSTREAM... UNTIL IT COMES *TOO CLOSE* TO A PLANET OR SUN!

WE'RE GONNA BE CAUGHT BETWEEN THE *COMET'S* PULL AND THAT WORLD'S *GRAVITATIONAL FORCE!* IT COULD GO *EITHER* WAY.

OR *BOTH!*

As the comet passes near the looming planet...

THE GRAVITATION PULL IS CAUSING THE COMET TO *FRAGMENT*, SIR!

STRAP IN, THREEPIO! THIS IS OUR CHANCE TO BREAK FREE OF THE COMET'S *SLIPSTREAM!*

IF WE'RE NOT *TORN APART!*

Hitting full power...

...Luke maneuvers his ship to be pulled from the comet's tail...into what is now a *METEORITE SHOWER* hurtling below!

Hurled and buffeted amid the fiery meteorite shower, Luke makes the only landing he can...

...a *BAD ONE!*

S-SIR...IS IT *OVER?* ARE WE *SAFE?!*

WE'VE SURVIVED THE *CRASH,* THREEPIO...BUT FROM THE SUDDEN DROP IN *TEMPERATURE,* I CAN'T GUARANTEE ANYTHING *ELSE!*

SIR, NO WONDER YOU FEEL *COLD...* THIS APPEARS TO BE A VIRTUAL *ICE PLANET!*

WE'RE IN *TROUBLE,* THREEPIO*!*

ANYTHING THOSE IMPERIALS WE ESCAPED *DIDN'T* KNOCK OUT...THIS CRASH *HAS!*

NO COMMUNICATOR... NO POWER... *NO HEAT!*

THIS *THERMAL GEAR* FROM THE EMERGENCY LOCKER IS *TEMPORARY* PROTECTION, BUT FROM THE LOOK OF THAT *SKY,* THE *WORST* IS STILL TO COME!

SIR, MY SENSORS INDICATE A STEADY AND *RAPID* DECLINE IN TEMPERATURE...*NIGHT* IS APPROACHING, I FEAR*!*

MORE THAN NIGHT, THREEPIO... LOOK ON THE *HORIZON!*

STORM CLOUDS! WE'VE GOT A *BLIZZARD* COMING OUR WAY... *FAST!*

EVEN WRECKED, THE SHIP IS *SOME* SHELTER, MASTER LUKE...

...SURELY, WITH YOUR *THERMAL GEAR,* YOU CAN WEATHER *WHATEVER* THIS DREADFUL ICEWORLD HURLS AT US!

WE'LL FIND OUT *SOON,* THREEPIO!

ONE BRIGHT NOTE, SIR...IT ISN'T LIKELY THE *EMPIRE* WILL COME LOOKING FOR US *HERE!*

Screaming winds descend on Luke and Threepio's wrecked spacecraft, carrying blinding snow and ice... and ever-dropping temperatures!

WE COULD BE *MUCH* WORSE OFF, SIR...SUPPOSE THE COMET HAD ACTUALLY *STRUCK* THIS MISERABLE SNOWBALL OF A WORLD...

...INSTEAD OF NARROWLY *MISSING* IT?

T-THIS IS OUR LAST... EMERGENCY *HEAT CAPSULE!* AFTER I-IT GOES...

...DON'T KNOW... H-HOW MUCH LONGER... I'LL BE AROUND, THREEPIO!

THE EXTREME COLD MUST BE PLAYING *HAVOC* WITH MY SENSOR CIRCUITRY...

...I COULD *SWEAR* I DETECTED SOMETHING *MOVING* OUTSIDE! PERHAPS *YOU* SHOULD TAKE A LOOK, MASTER LUKE...

MASTER LUKE!

THE LAST *HEAT CAPSULE* IS *EXHAUSTED!* MASTER LUKE HAS *SUCCUMBED* TO THIS AWFUL *COLD!*

THERE MUST BE *SOMETHING* I CAN DO...BUT *WHAT?!*

The watcher stares intently at the unconscious Luke Skywalker...

...then turns into the raging ice storm...

...to *DEPART!*

Then...

...she abruptly wheels her mount...and rushes *BACK!*

Threepio bends helplessly over his nearly frozen Master...

...unaware of being watched from outside their wrecked starship!

BY THE ORIGINAL MAKER! *WHO*?!

NO *QUESTIONS*, DROID! LIFT YOUR MASTER... OUR LIVES *DEPEND* ON MOVING SWIFTLY!

Threepio follows his unexpected rescuer's orders...

WHAT *IS* THE CREATURE MASTER LUKE IS ON?

A *TAUNTAUN!* BUT EVEN IT CAN'T SURVIVE A *NIGHT STORM* ON HOTH!

HOTH! THAT'S THIS DREADFUL *PLANET?*

YES! AND IF WE SURVIVE THE WORST *IT* CAN THROW...WE STILL HAVE TO FACE MY *FATHER'S* WRATH!

The girl leads Threepio and the unconscious Luke through the storm's fury, until...

UNLESS MY PHOTO-RECEPTORS *DECEIVE* ME, THERE'S A *LIGHT* AHEAD!

MY *HOME*, SEE-THREEPIO, UNFORTUNATELY...

...YOU AND YOUR HANDSOME YOUNG MASTER MUST NOW FACE THE WRATH OF MY *FATHER!*

FRIJA! WHAT HAVE YOU *DONE?!* HAVEN'T I ALWAYS SAID OUR SAFETY AND HAPPINESS HERE ON *HOTH* DEPEND ON *NO ONE* DISCOVERING OUR PRESENCE?

SCRAP THE DROID FOR *PARTS*... RETURN THE HUMAN TO THE *ELEMENTS!*

As *IMPERIAL GOVERNOR*, I found it best to deal *RUTHLESSLY* with small problems...before they become *BIG* ones!

FATHER, I WON'T LET YOU *HARM* THIS DROID *OR* HIS MASTER! THEY'VE CRASHED ON HOTH AS *WE* DID...THEY'RE NO *THREAT!*

I *NEED* THE COMPANY OF SOMEONE MY OWN *AGE!* SOMEONE YOUNG...ATTRACTIVE...

YOU'RE TALKING *NONSENSE*, FRIJA...

...OUR SURVIVAL DEPENDS ON REMAINING *ALONE! ASIDE*, NOW! TRUST ME TO *ELIMINATE* THIS PROBLEM AS AN IMPERIAL GOVERNOR SHOULD!

OUR SAFETY *CANNOT* BE IMPERILED FOR THE SAKE OF SOME HALF-FROZEN YOUNG *FOOL!*

HE'S HAD A CHANCE TO *THAW*, MR. IMPERIAL GOVERNOR!

Revived but weakened, Luke finds Frija's father a surprisingly strong and agile opponent....!

YOUR EFFORTS GAINED YOU *ONE* THING, MY OVER-EAGER YOUNG TROUBLEMAKER... DEATH BY *BLASTER* INSTEAD OF BEING LEFT TO SLOWLY *FREEZE* IN HOTH'S *NIGHT STORMS!*

Before Frija's father can fire... Luke's arm swings up from his side with dazzling swiftness!

W-WHAT...?!

A *LIGHTSABER*...WEAPON OF THE *JEDI KNIGHTS!* FUNNY...I'D THINK YOU WERE THE RIGHT AGE TO *REMEMBER* THEM!

THREEPIO, FIND THEIR *COMMUNICATOR* AND SIGNAL FOR *HELP!*

YOU'LL FIND THAT *IMPOSSIBLE,* MY YOUNG HERO... YOU'RE *STRANDED* ON HOTH!

A FEW QUICK BLEEPS ON OUR EMERGENCY SIGNAL FREQUENCY WILL BRING *HELP* WITHOUT ALERTING THE *EMPIRE!*

YOUNG FOOL...THERE'S NO DANGER OF ALERTING ANYONE!

PART 13

I'VE FOUND THEIR *COMMUNICATOR*, SIR! ONLY... IT'S AS HOPELESSLY DAMAGED AS THE ONE IN *OUR* WRECKED SHIP!

ALL YOUR *OTHER* EQUIPMENT IS OKAY...I THINK YOU'VE *DELIBERATELY* ISOLATED YOURSELF ON HOTH, MR. IMPERIAL GOVERNOR!

AND YOU'VE *JOINED* US... AGAINST MY WILL!

HE COULD HAVE *KILLED* YOU AND DIDN'T... THAT *PROVES* LUKE'S NOT DANGEROUS!

HIS MERE *ARRIVAL* HAS TURNED *YOU* AGAINST ME, CHILD. I DESERTED THE *EMPIRE* TO *SAVE* US...

...AND LETTING MERE *LONELINESS* ATTRACT YOU TO THIS YOUNG FOOL IS GOING TO *RUIN* THAT!

LOCK HIM *UP*, THREEPIO! I'VE GOT AN *IDEA*...

MORNING! Luke *ACTS* on his idea...

WHY DIDN'T YOUR FATHER SEEK REFUGE WITH THE *REBEL ALLIANCE*, FRIJA?

H-HE... HATES *BOTH* SIDES!

HE'S SURE *SERIOUS* ABOUT ISOLATING THE TWO OF YOU FROM THE EMPIRE *AND* THE REBELLION... BUT I THINK I'VE GOT A *SOLUTION* TO THE PROBLEM...

...ESPECIALLY SINCE THREEPIO LOCKED HIM AWAY WHERE HE CAN'T *INTERFERE!*"

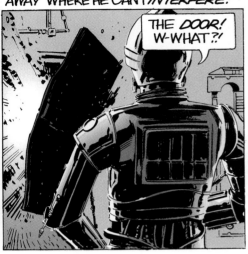

THE *DOOR!* W-WHAT?!

LUKE, I'M WILLING TO DEFY MY FATHER TO *HELP* YOU, EXCEPT... WHAT CAN WE DO *HERE?*

YEAH, MY SHIP'S COMMUNICATOR IS AS USELESS AS *YOURS!* HOWEVER...

...*BETWEEN* THE TWO, I BET WE CAN CANNIBALIZE ENOUGH PARTS FOR A *WORKING MODEL!*

But... GOVERNOR! YOU'RE *FREE!* BUT HOW--

YOUR YOUNG MASTER DESTROYED *ONE* OF MY WEAPONS! I KEEP *OTHERS* SECRETED *THROUGHOUT* THE ICE CAVE!

THAT *DOES* IT, FRIJA! WITH THE PARTS WE'VE SALVAGED FROM THIS WRECK'S COMMUNICATOR, *COMBINED* WITH THE DAMAGED ONE BACK AT YOUR CAVE...

...I'M *SURE* I'LL BE SIGNALLING THE *REBEL ALLIANCE* IN NO TIME!

IT'S *WONDERFUL* WORKING WITH YOU, LUKE! ACTUALLY SHARING SOME *PURPOSE*...

...INSTEAD OF JUST *EXISTING* IN ISOLATION DAY AFTER DAY, AS MY *FATHER* INSISTS WE DO!

HOTH IS A GREAT PLACE FOR HIDING FROM THE *EMPIRE*, FRIJA....

...BUT FOR A YOUNG GIRL LIKE YOU TO BE *ISOLATED* HERE IS--

HER *FATHER'S* BUSINESS, SKYWALKER! WHICH YOU'VE INTERFERED IN FOR THE *LAST TIME!*

FATHER, LEAVE US *ALONE!* I'M *HAPPY* HELPING LUKE!

HE'LL SOON BRING HIS REBEL FRIENDS *SWARMING*, FRIJA...

...AND THE *IMPERIALS* WON'T BE FAR BEHIND! THE WAR I DESERTED THE EMPIRE TO *SAVE* US FROM WILL BE RIGHT HERE ON HOTH!

I *KNEW* THE DAY WOULD COME WHEN REBELS *OR* IMPERIALS WOULD THREATEN OUR *SAFETY* HERE!

YOU'LL *THANK* ME FOR THIS LATER, CHILD!

NO!

FRIJA! YOU ALMOST TOOK THAT BLAST MEANT FOR *ME!*

GET THAT TAUNTAUN WITH THE COMMUNICATOR PARTS BACK TO *THREEPIO!*

I DON'T KNOW WHERE THE GOVERNOR GOT THAT BLASTER... BUT IT'S *ME* HE WANTS, NOT YOU!

GET *OUT* OF HERE, FRIJA! I'LL DRAW YOUR FATHER'S FIRE!

CANNIBALIZED *PARTS*? THE COMMUNICATOR I WRECKED AT THE CAVE CAN BE *REPAIRED* WITH THEM! UNLESS...

The one-time Imperial Governor takes hasty aim...

But...

FRIJA! I-I MEANT TO HIT THE TAUNTAUN WITH THE PACK!

YOU WANTED TO KEEP HER *CUT OFF* ON THIS PLANET SO BADLY YOU *KILLED* HER!

SKYWALKER! IT'S *YOUR* FAULT MY DAUGHTER TURNED AGAINST ME! IT'S *YOUR* FAULT I HAD TO SHOOT HER...

AND NOW YOU'LL *DIE* FOR IT!

Frija's raging father squeezes the blaster trigger...

The lightsaber stroke *FELLS* Frija's father...

HIS BLASTER *JERKED* AS IT FIRED...INSTEAD OF SHATTERING *IT.* I GOT THE *GOVERNOR!* H-HE'S...

...and Luke has no choice but to *STRIKE!*

HE'S...SOME KIND OF *MECHANICAL CREATION!* AN ELABORATE SORT OF... *DROID!*

L-LUKE!

FRIJA! I NEVER MEANT FOR *ANYTHING* TO HAPPEN TO YOU OR YOUR FATHER...

DON'T BLAME YOURSELF, LUKE! WE'RE *BOTH* MECHANICAL... CREATED BY *IMPERIAL TECHNICIANS!*

WE WERE DESIGNED TO BE *DECOYS*-- PROGRAMMED TO IMITATE THE *REAL* GOVERNOR AND HIS DAUGHTER--SO *THEY* COULD FLEE A REBEL ATTACK!

PERHAPS WE WERE PROGRAMMED *TOO* PERFECTLY! MY FATHER'S SURVIVAL INSTINCTS WERE SO *STRONG*...HE HAD *US* ESCAPE INSTEAD!

THE EMPIRE DESIGNED MY FATHER AND ME TO BE *TARGETS* FOR THE *REBELS*...THAT'S WHY HE HATED *BOTH* SIDES!

AND IF I HADN'T *CRASHED* HERE, FRIJA...

...THE TWO OF YOU WOULD BE LIVING SAFELY AND HAPPILY!

NO...MERELY *EXISTING*! AND WE WEREN'T CREATED TO LAST *LONG*...

YOU BROUGHT *PURPOSE* AND *ENJOYMENT* TO THE TIME I HAD. DON'T *REGRET* WHAT HAPPENED HERE, LUKE...

...I *THANK* YOU FOR IT!

REBUILD THE COMMUNICATOR AND SUMMON YOUR *FRIENDS*, LUKE. I'M SORRY MY FATHER *FOUGHT* SO AGAINST YOU...

...BUT I'M *GLAD* YOU CAME TO HOTH!

FOR THE CHANCE TO HAVE KNOWN *YOU*, FRIJA, SO AM I...SO AM *I*!

MASTER LUKE! THE SNOW KEPT ME FROM REACHING YOU *QUICKLY!* I *KNOW* THE GOVERNOR HAD A *BLASTER!* DID HE...?

...ACCIDENTLY SHOT *FRIJA,* THREEPIO! ALMOST GOT *ME* TOO...MY *LIGHTSABER* STOPPED HIM!

THANKS TO FRIJA, WE'LL *LEAVE* HOTH SOON, THREEPIO. THANKS *ALSO* TO HER... IT'S A PLACE I'LL *NEVER* FORGET!

THE STARSHIP YARDS OF FONDOR! Space tugs and equipment barges barely have time to scatter...

...as an awesome creation *ROARS* into life!

GENTLEMEN... A *TOAST!* TO CELEBRATE *COMPLETION* OF THE MOST POWERFUL NEW CRAFT IN THE IMPERIAL FLEET!

NO!

I'VE A MORE *PRACTICAL* CELEBRATION IN MIND!

START ALL ENGINES!

L-LORD VADER... OUR *DESTINATION?*

THE *NEAREST* INSTALLATION OF THE *REBEL ALLIANCE!* WE'RE GOING TO *CHRISTEN* OUR SHIP!

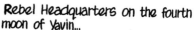

Rebel Headquarters on the fourth moon of Yavin...

BREE-DOOOT! BREE-DOOOT!

HEY...!

SOMEBODY OUGHT'A *TELL* THAT HALF-PINT HE'S AN ASTRO-DROID... NOT A *LANDSPEEDER!*

ARTOO'S JUST *EXCITED,* HAN... WE'VE *HEARD* FROM LUKE AND THREEPIO! THEY'RE *SAFE!*

LUKE AND THREEPIO JUST *NOW* MANAGED TO REPAIR THEIR COMMUNICATOR AFTER CRASHING ON A PLANET CALLED *HOTH!*

GOTTA GIVE THE KID *CREDIT...*

...HE'S FOUND A PLACE EVEN *I* CAN'T RECALL!

THEN THE *EMPIRE* CERTAINLY WON'T KNOW, HAN! LUKE THINKS IT COULD SERVE AS OUR *NEW BASE!*

But elsewhere...

OUR *DEFENSE SHIELD* IS SHATTERED!

WE NEVER HAD A *CHANCE!* WARN *YAVIN* BASE... *WARN YAVIN!*

PRINCESS LEIA! CAPTAIN SOLO! THERE'S AN *EMERGENCY MEETING!* WE'VE HAD *DISASTROUS NEWS* FROM LAAKTEEN DEPOT!

The Rebel high command gathers in emergency session...

...OUR COURSE IS CLEAR! PRINCESS LEIA, ONCE *SKYWALKER* REJOINS YOU...

...YOU *MUST* SECURE THE HELP OF THE *MON CALAMARI!*

THERE'S NO *MISTAKE?* WE FOUGHT NEARLY A *YEAR* TO WIN LAAKTEEN DEPOT!

"AS OF NOW," says General Dodonna, "IT DOESN'T *EXIST!*"

I CHRISTEN THIS SHIP... *THE EXECUTOR!*

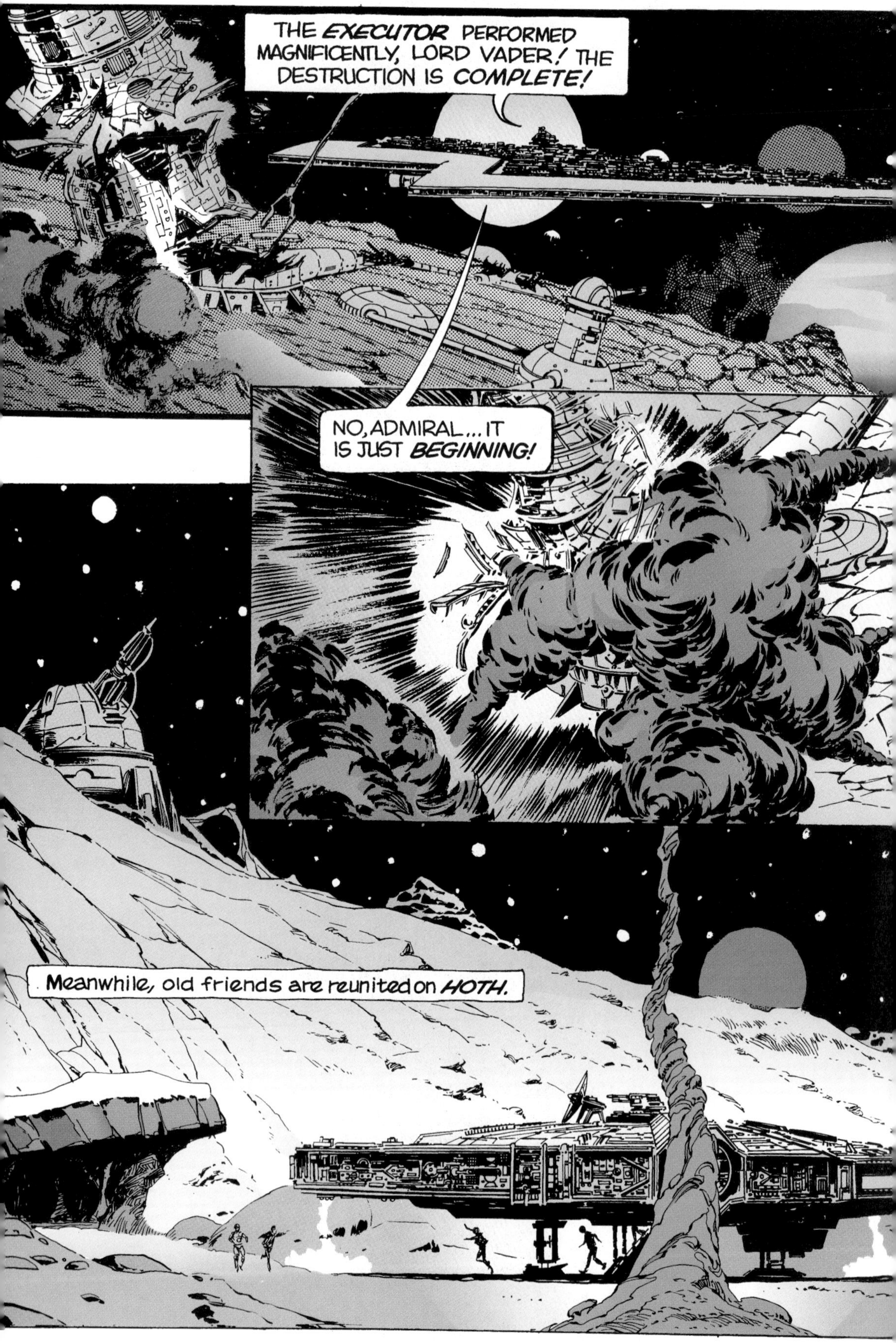

THE *EXECUTOR* PERFORMED MAGNIFICENTLY, LORD VADER! THE DESTRUCTION IS *COMPLETE!*
NO, ADMIRAL... IT IS JUST *BEGINNING!*
Meanwhile, old friends are reunited on *HOTH.*

I *KNEW* ONCE THREEPIO AND I GOT A *COMMUNICATOR* WORKING AGAIN...WE'D GET OFF THIS *SNOWBALL* FAST!

KID, YOU'LL BE SEEING A *LOT* OF THIS "SNOWBALL..."

...THE ALLIANCE BRASS *LIKE* YOUR SUGGESTION OF MAKING *THIS* THEIR NEW BASE!

The *MILLENNIUM FALCON* departs after picking up Luke and Threepio...

YOU COULDN'T ASK FOR A MORE *ISOLATED* SPOT TO HIDE FROM THE EMPIRE...

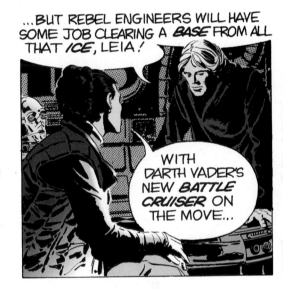

...BUT REBEL ENGINEERS WILL HAVE SOME JOB CLEARING A *BASE* FROM ALL THAT *ICE*, LEIA!

WITH DARTH VADER'S NEW *BATTLE CRUISER* ON THE MOVE...

...*EVERYONE'S* WORK IS CUT OUT FOR THEM! TO SUCCESSFULLY EVACUATE OUR *YAVIN HEADQUARTERS* REQUIRES HELP...SO WE'RE SEEKING OUT THE *MON CALAMARI!*

THE *WHO?*

THE *MON CALAMARI* HAVE WAGED THEIR OWN BATTLE AGAINST THE EMPIRE FOR SOME TIME, LUKE...NOW THEY'VE JOINED THE *REBEL ALLIANCE!*

TO EVACUATE OUR YAVIN HEADQUARTERS, WE NEED A *DIVERSION* FOR THE IMPERIALS... I'M MEETING WITH THE MON CALAMARI LEADER, *ADMIRAL ACKBAR*, TO SEE IF *THEY* CAN SUPPLY IT!

BETTER *STRAP IN* BACK THERE, PRINCESS! WE'RE APPROACHING OUR *RENDEZVOUS COORDINATES*...TIME TO DROP FROM *HYPERSPACE!*

The *MILLENNIUM FALCON* pops out of hyperspace...

THE *HAN SOLO* DELIVERY SERVICE DOES IT AGAIN, YOUR WORSHIP! THIS IS YOUR *RENDEZVOUS SPOT!*

THEN WHY DON'T WE SEE *ADMIRAL ACKBAR'S* SHIP?

WE HIT THE COORDINATES *PERFECTLY!* MAYBE BEIN' ON *TIME* IS AGAINST THE MON CALAMARI *CODE!* MAYBE--*UH-OH!*

HAN! THAT *DEBRIS*...THERE'S BEEN A *BATTLE* HERE!

WORSE THAN THAT, PRINCESS... IT LOOKS LIKE YOUR ALLY, ADMIRAL ACKBAR, *LOST!*

CAN YOU BE *SURE* THIS BATTLE DEBRIS WAS ADMIRAL ACKBAR'S SHIP, HAN? HE WAS TRAVELING IN AN ARMED *BULK FREIGHTER* TO THROW OFF THE EMPIRE!

I'M AFRAID IT DIDN'T *WORK,* LEIA...

THAT'S DEFINITELY THE *REMAINS* OF A BULK FREIGHTER *BRIDGE SECTION* AHEAD!

HAN, OUR HOPES FOR SUCCESSFULLY EVACUATING THE YAVIN BASE BEFORE *DARTH VADER* STRIKES DEPEND ON MON CALAMARI *SUPPORT!*

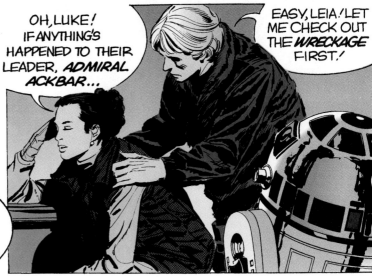

OH, LUKE! IF ANYTHING'S HAPPENED TO THEIR LEADER, *ADMIRAL ACKBAR...*

EASY, LEIA! LET ME CHECK OUT THE *WRECKAGE* FIRST!

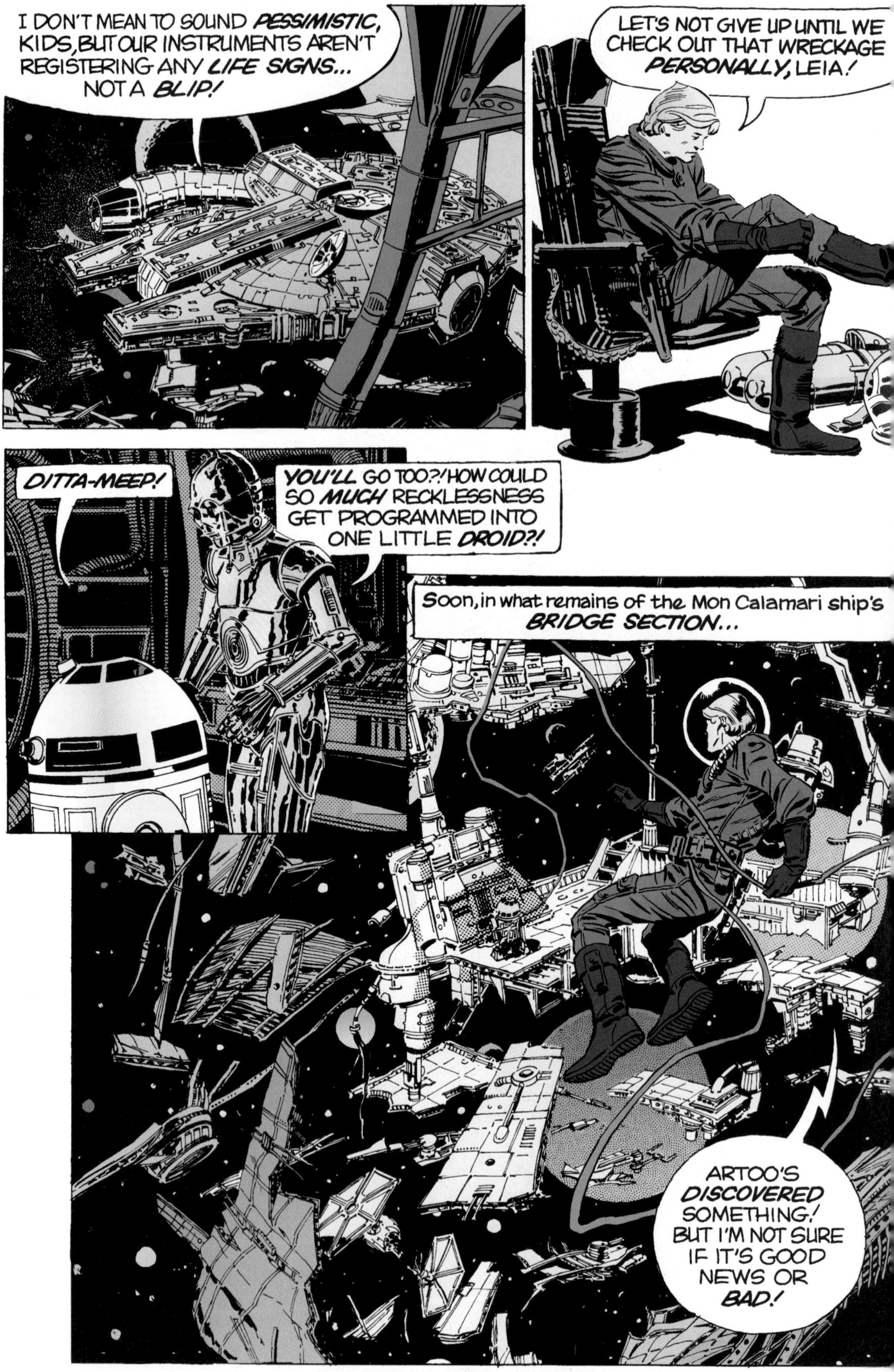

I DON'T MEAN TO SOUND PESSIMISTIC, KIDS, BUT OUR INSTRUMENTS AREN'T REGISTERING ANY LIFE SIGNS... NOT A BLIP!
LET'S NOT GIVE UP UNTIL WE CHECK OUT THAT WRECKAGE PERSONALLY, LEIA!
DITTA-MEEP!
YOU'LL GO TOO?! HOW COULD SO MUCH RECKLESSNESS GET PROGRAMMED INTO ONE LITTLE DROID?!
Soon, in what remains of the Mon Calamari ship's BRIDGE SECTION...
ARTOO'S DISCOVERED SOMETHING! BUT I'M NOT SURE IF IT'S GOOD NEWS OR BAD!

THE LITTLE GUY'S DREDGED *SOMETHING* UP FROM ONE OF THE RUINED COMPUTERS...

Aboard the *MILLENNIUM FALCON*, See-Threepio translates...

THE MACHINE APPARENTLY RECORDED THE LAUNCHING OF SEVERAL *ESCAPE PODS* INSTANTS BEFORE IMPERIAL FIRE EXPLODED THE VESSEL!

HAN, IS THERE A *PLANET* NEAR ENOUGH FOR THOSE PODS TO REACH?

IF THE *EMPIRE* DIDN'T REACH THE PODS *FIRST*, YOUR ROYALNESS!

NAVICOMPUTER SHOWS A WORLD CALLED *DALUUJ* WITHIN ESCAPE-POD RANGE!

THEN ADMIRAL ACKBAR COULD *BE* THERE, HAN!

NO *GUARANTEES*, PRINCESS... A *LOT* MIGHT 'VE GONE WRONG!

AT LEAST THERE'S *HOPE!* THE MON CALAMARI LOSING THEIR *LEADER* AT THIS PARTICULAR TIME...

...IS A SETBACK FROM WHICH *THEY* AND THE ENTIRE *REBEL ALLIANCE* MIGHT NOT RECOVER!

MAGNETIZE THAT STUBBY LITTLE BODY, ARTOO-DETOO!

ATMOSPHERIC CONDITIONS ON DALUUJ ARE OBVIOUSLY TOO *UNSTABLE* FOR YOU TO GO ROLLING AROUND *LOOSE*...

LUKE, TELL EVERYBODY THEY CAN *RELAX* BACK THERE IN THE MAIN CABIN...WE'RE DROPPIN' DOWN NEAR THE *SURFACE!* IT'LL BE MUCH *SMOOTHER!*

HAN SOLO! W-WHAT...?!

SORRY ABOUT THAT, YOUR WORSHIP! VISIBILITY'S A BIT *TRICKY* DOWN HERE...

...WE JUST HAD A *NEAR MISS* WITH WHAT SEEMS TO BE THE *GUN TURRET* OF AN *IMPERIAL FORT!* BUT NO BIG DEAL...

...WE CAME IN SO *LOW* AND *FAST*, I DOUBT THEY COULD *TRACK* US...

BUT COULD THEY TRACK THOSE *ESCAPE PODS* OF OUR MON CALAMARI ALLIES?!

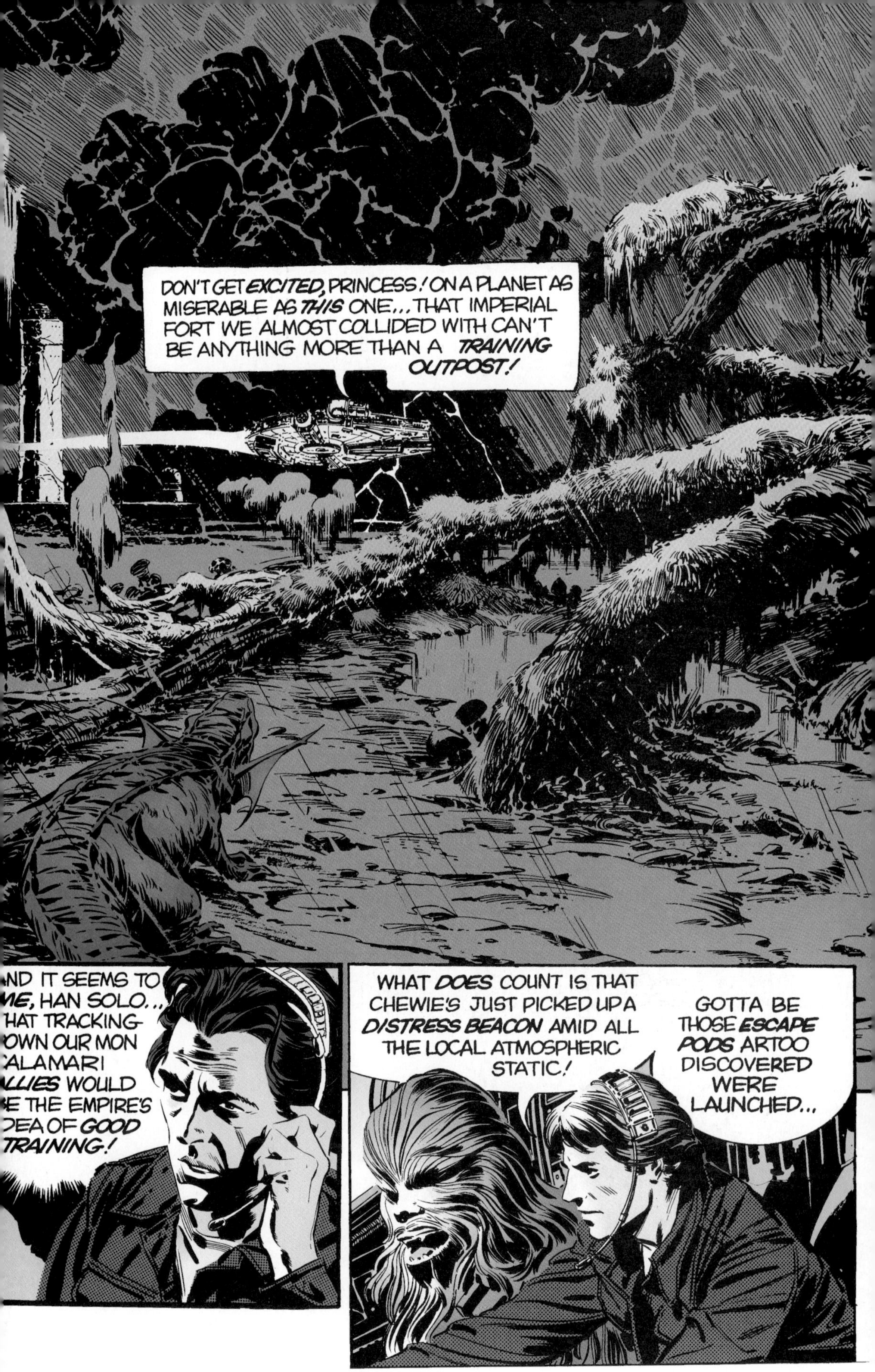
DON'T GET EXCITED, PRINCESS! ON A PLANET AS MISERABLE AS THIS ONE... THAT IMPERIAL FORT WE ALMOST COLLIDED WITH CAN'T BE ANYTHING MORE THAN A TRAINING OUTPOST!
ND IT SEEMS TO ME, HAN SOLO... HAT TRACKING-OWN OUR MON ALAMARI LLIES WOULD E THE EMPIRE'S DEA OF GOOD TRAINING!
WHAT DOES COUNT IS THAT CHEWIE'S JUST PICKED UP A DISTRESS BEACON AMID ALL THE LOCAL ATMOSPHERIC STATIC!
GOTTA BE THOSE ESCAPE PODS ARTOO DISCOVERED WERE LAUNCHED...

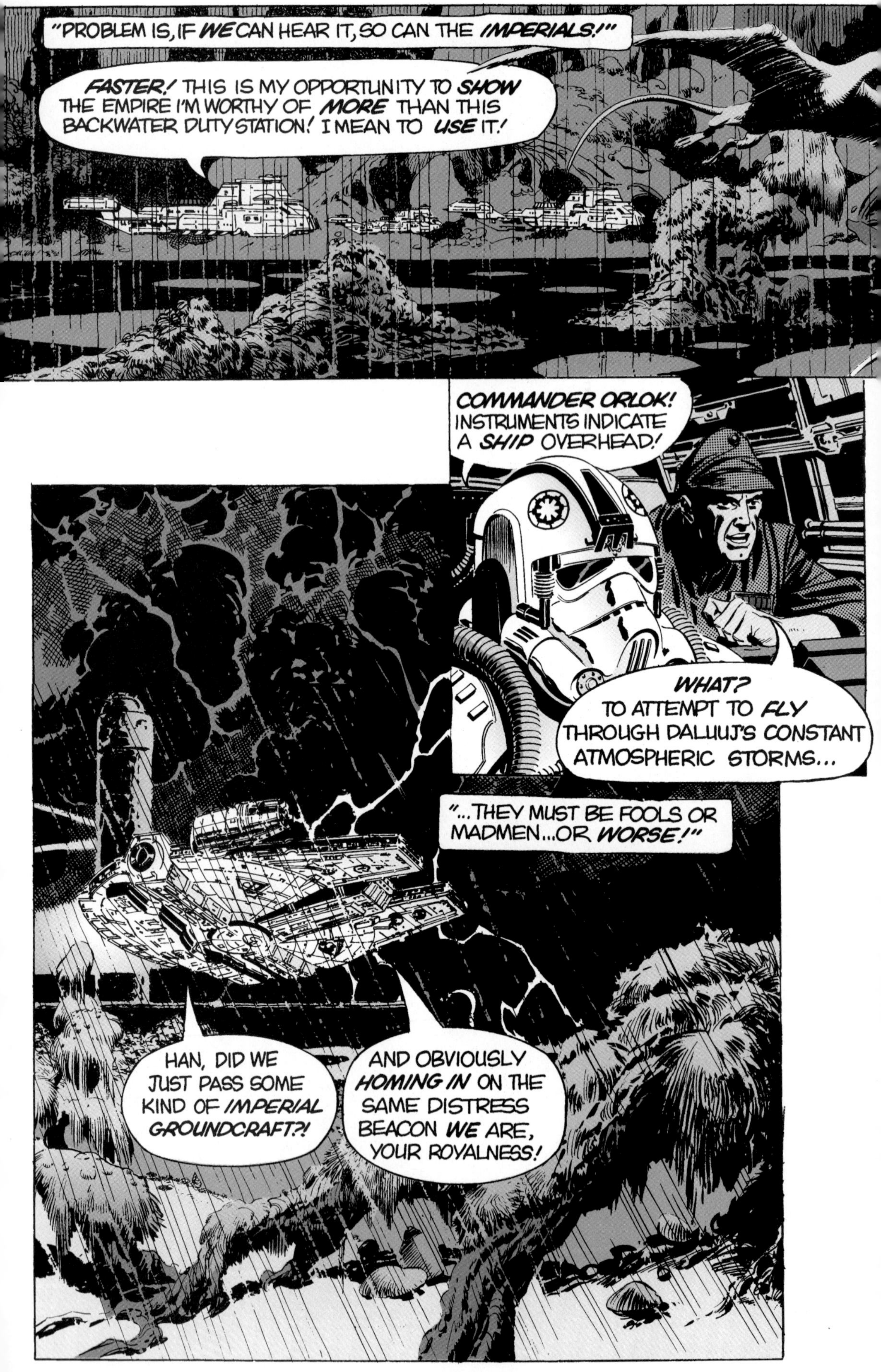

"PROBLEM IS, IF WE CAN HEAR IT, SO CAN THE IMPERIALS!"
FASTER! THIS IS MY OPPORTUNITY TO SHOW THE EMPIRE I'M WORTHY OF MORE THAN THIS BACKWATER DUTY STATION! I MEAN TO USE IT!
COMMANDER ORLOK! INSTRUMENTS INDICATE A SHIP OVERHEAD!
WHAT? TO ATTEMPT TO FLY THROUGH DALUUJ'S CONSTANT ATMOSPHERIC STORMS...
"...THEY MUST BE FOOLS OR MADMEN...OR WORSE!"
HAN, DID WE JUST PASS SOME KIND OF IMPERIAL GROUNDCRAFT?!
AND OBVIOUSLY HOMING IN ON THE SAME DISTRESS BEACON WE ARE, YOUR ROYALNESS!

TELL THE OTHER PILOTS *FULL SPEED!* CLEARLY WE ARE IN A *RACE* TOWARD THE SOURCE OF THAT BEACON!

THE EMPIRE *STUCK* ME ON THIS STORM-SWEPT EXCUSE FOR A WORLD...I'M GOING TO *PROVE* I'M WORTHY OF FAR, *FAR* MORE THAN RUNNING A TRAINING STATION!

IF BY SOME MIRACLE THEY SURVIVE TO *LAND,* I MEAN TO SEE THEY *NEVER* TAKE OFF! THIS VENTURE WILL BE MY TICKET *AWAY* FROM DALUUJ!

Ahead...

COME FORWARD, LEIA! LOOK THERE... ON THAT HIGH GROUND!

HAN! I THINK IT'S *ADMIRAL ACKBAR* AND HIS PEOPLE!

IT *IS* ACKBAR, HAN! I RECOGNIZE HIS ADMIRAL'S UNIFORM!

NO WAY WE CAN *HOVER* IN THIS STORM, PRINCESS! GOT TO SET DOWN ON THAT *MUD PLAIN* NEAR YOUR MON CALAMARI BUDDIES!

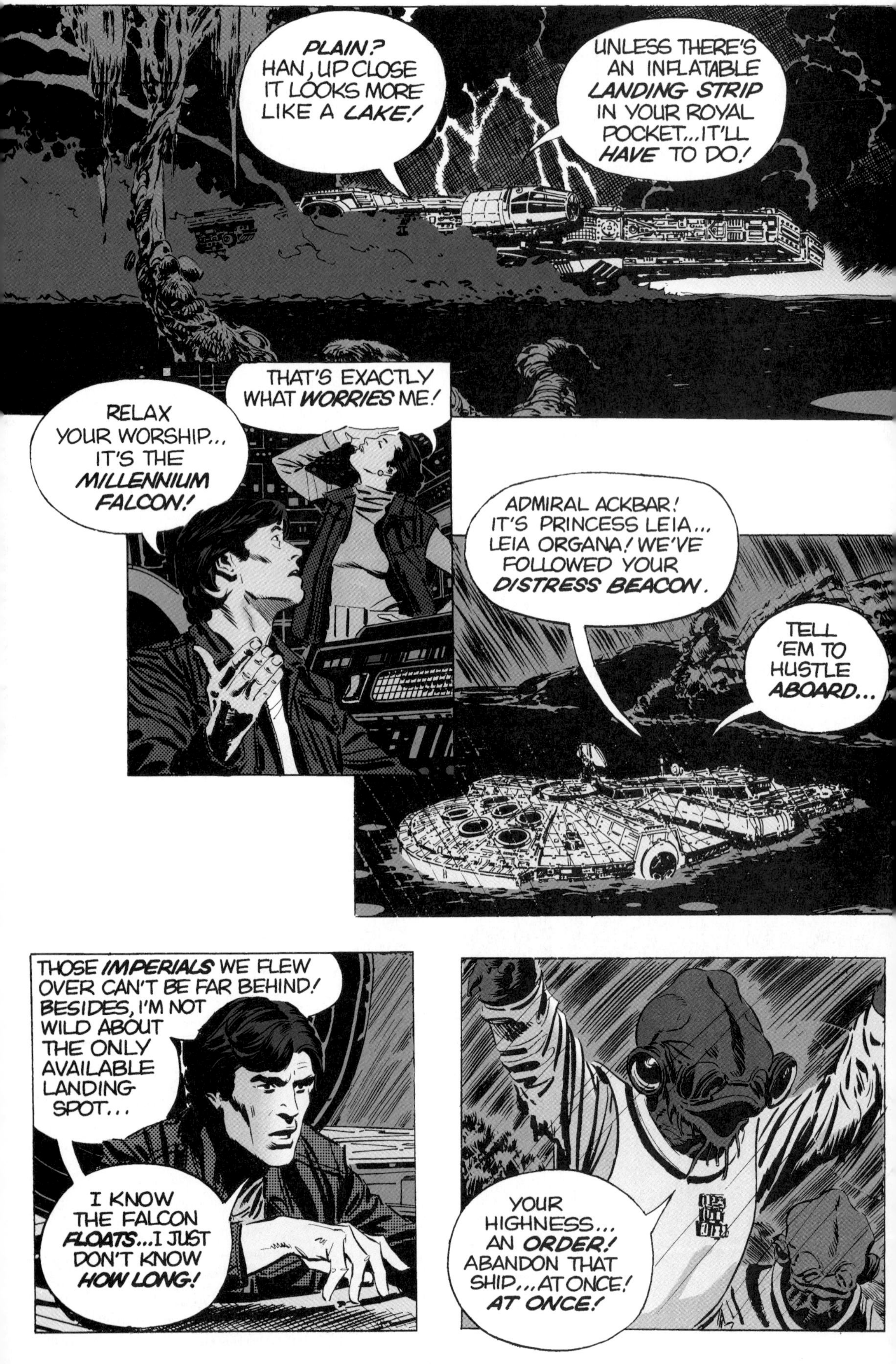
PLAIN? HAN, UP CLOSE IT LOOKS MORE LIKE A LAKE!
UNLESS THERE'S AN INFLATABLE LANDING STRIP IN YOUR ROYAL POCKET...IT'LL HAVE TO DO!
RELAX YOUR WORSHIP... IT'S THE MILLENNIUM FALCON!
THAT'S EXACTLY WHAT WORRIES ME!
ADMIRAL ACKBAR! IT'S PRINCESS LEIA... LEIA ORGANA! WE'VE FOLLOWED YOUR DISTRESS BEACON.
TELL 'EM TO HUSTLE ABOARD...
THOSE IMPERIALS WE FLEW OVER CAN'T BE FAR BEHIND! BESIDES, I'M NOT WILD ABOUT THE ONLY AVAILABLE LANDING SPOT...
I KNOW THE FALCON FLOATS...I JUST DON'T KNOW HOW LONG!
YOUR HIGHNESS... AN ORDER! ABANDON THAT SHIP...AT ONCE! AT ONCE!

HUH?! I KNOW YOU HAD TO BE A *LITTLE* NUTS TO JOIN THE REBEL ALLIANCE...

...BUT YOUR ADMIRAL BUDDY IS *OVERDOING* IT! AND I-- YEOOW!

Joined by the Mon Calamari, Han and Leia swim to free those still caught on the *MILLENNIUM FALCON!* One by one, they appear! Except...

MASTER LUKE! WHERE'S *ARTOO?!*

WHAT *ARE* THOSE THINGS?! WHAT ARE THEY DOING TO *MY* SHIP?!

THEY DRAG IT *UNDER!* YOUR FRIENDS *WITH* IT... IF WE DO NOT *ACT!*

But as the coiling, twining creatures drag the struggling ship beneath the murky waters...

...there is **NO SIGN** of the little droid!

I'D DO **ANYTHING** TO BRING THE LITTLE FELLOW BACK! **ANYTHING!**

I SUGGEST YOUR 3PO UNIT TRY **SILENCE**, PRINCESS! MY MEN CALL ABOUT A **DISCOVERY!**

YOUR **OTHER** DROID! STUCK IN THE SHALLOWS... SOMETHING HEAVY **CLINGS** TO IT!

THE **WORMS** ARE TRYING TO DRAG HIM BACK! **SAVE** HIM, ADMIRAL ACKBAR!

The little astro-droid is hauled from the mud lake!

NO WONDER HE WAS **STUC** HE'S MAGNETIZE A **SUPPLY LOCKER** TO H HOUSING,

ARE YOUR **LOGIC CIRCUITS** CORRODED, ARTOO?! YOU'RE LUCKY YOU DIDN'T **SINK** WITH THE **MILLENNIUM FALCON!**

IT WON'T BE SUNK **LONG!** GIMME YOUR **LIGHTSABER**, LUKE!

I DON'T CARE **HOW** BIG THEY ARE... NO CRUMMY **WORMS** ARE GONNA STEAL **MY** SHIP!

HAN!

PERHAPS YOU CAN FIGHT THE WORM GIANTS *ALONE*, CAPTAIN...

...BUT CAN YOU ALSO BREATHE *MUD*?!

"OKAY, MAYBE I'M LEAPIN' BEFORE I *THINK*, ADMIRAL ACKBAR! BUT WITHOUT THE *FALCON*...

"...THE ONLY *OTHER* RIDES AROUND ARE GONNA COME COURTESY OF THE *EMPIRE*!"

HAVING WORMS EAT THE *MILLENNIUM FALCON* ISN'T OUR ONLY PROBLEM, ADMIRAL ACKBAR! WE PASSED *IMPERIAL GROUNDCRAFT* ON OUR WAY TO *FINDING* YOU.

NOT *EATEN*...YOUR *MILLENNIUM FALCON* WAS MERELY HAULED TO THE MUD LAKE'S *BOTTOM!* ESCAPE PODS WHICH CARRIED ME...MY MEN... SUFFERED THE *SAME!*

THOSE GIANT WORMS GOT YOUR *ESCAPE PODS* JUST LIKE THEY DID THE *FALCON*, ADMIRAL ACKBAR?

AND YOU DIDN'T *DO* ANYTHING?!

DEBATE SEEMED WASTED ON THE CREATURES, CAPTAIN SOLO. BLASTER FIRE, *INEFFECTIVE*...

OBVIOUSLY, *ACTION* IS NEEDED... SHALL WE EXAMINE THE *SUPPLY LOCKER* YOUR R2 UNIT SALVAGED?

SPACE ARMOR... REPAIR TORCHES... YOUR HALF-PINT DROID SAVED THE *RIGHT* SUPPLY LOCKER, LUKE! AND I'M PUTTIN' THIS STUFF TO *IMMEDIATE* USE!

RASH, CAPTAIN SOLO! I SUGGEST LEAVING MUD LAKE OPERATIONS TO ME... MY MEN! YOU, YOUR COMPANIONS, CAN--

YOU LEAD THE *MON CALAMARI,* ADMIRAL ACKBAR... NOT *ME!* THE *FALCON'S* MY SHIP... *I'M* GETTIN' IT AWAY FROM THOSE NIGHTMARE-SIZE WORMS!

Heedlessly, Han plunges into the mud lake's depths!

WHAT'S IT GONNA TAKE TO SHAKE THOSE SQUIRMIN' MONSTERS *OFF* HER?!

MAYBE A REPAIR TORCH *HOTFOOT* WILL-- *AGHHH!* WHAT'S *HAPPENING* TO ME?!

IT'S *HAN*, ADMIRAL ACKBAR! BUT HE WOULDN'T COME UP SO *QUICKLY* UNLESS--

SOMETHING IS *WRONG*, SKYWALKER! AND I HAVE SUSPICIONS *WHAT!*

WARRRGH?

S-SUIT WAS DESIGNED FOR *SPACE*, CHEWIE...PRESSURE'S *DIFFERENT* AT BOTTOM OF MUD LAKE! TOO MUCH FOR *ME*...EVEN *WITH* PROTECTION!

'FRAID WE'VE LOST... A *SHIP*, OL' BUDDY!

NOT *SO*... ONLY VALUABLE *TIME!*

WE MON CALAMARI ARE *AMPHIBIANS* CAPTAIN SOLO... BETTER SUITED TO THE MUD LAKE'S *PRESSURES* THAN YOU!

WISH YOU'D MENTIONED THAT *BEFORE* I DIVED TO ITS *BOTTOM!*

YOU DIDN'T EXACTLY GIVE ADMIRAL ACKBAR THE *CHANCE,* HAN!

AWRIGHT, AWRIGHT! BUT IT'S *TOUGH* DOIN' NOTHING WITH MY *SHIP* AT STAKE, LUKE!

HARDLY *NOTHING,* CAPTAIN! WHILE *WE* RAISE THE *MILLENNIUM FALCON,* YOU AND YOUR FRIENDS MUST *HOLD OFF* THE APPROACHING *IMPERIALS!*

THREE OF US AGAINST THREE ARMED SKIMMERS! *PERFECT* ODDS!

WILL YOU QUIT *COMPLAINING,* HAN! AT LEAST THE *RAIN'S* STOPPED!

YEAH! NOW WE'RE INTO DALUUJ'S *FOG SEASON!* IT'S JUST AS *WET*...BUT WE DON'T HAVE TO *SEE* HOW MISERABLE THIS PLANET IS!

MAYBE YOU SHOULD'VE SWITCHED *JOBS* WITH LEIA...

KID, TO AVOID *DISASTER* IN THIS SOUP...YOU NEED A *SMUGGLER'S* UNERRING INSTINCTS!

...SHE WASN'T *THRILLED* ABOUT DRAWING THE LOT TO STAY WITH THE DROIDS AND MAINTAIN A *FIX* ON US!

While the Star Warriors and their Mon Calamari allies make plans...

...their Imperial foes draw relentlessly *CLOSER!*

PART 14

WHILE HIS MON CALAMARI RAISE THE *FALCON,* ADMIRAL ACKBAR EXPECTS US TO *HOLD OFF* THE IMPERIALS! EVEN WITH *MY* NAVIGATIONAL INSTINCTS...

...WE'LL BE LUCKY TO EVEN *FIND* 'EM!

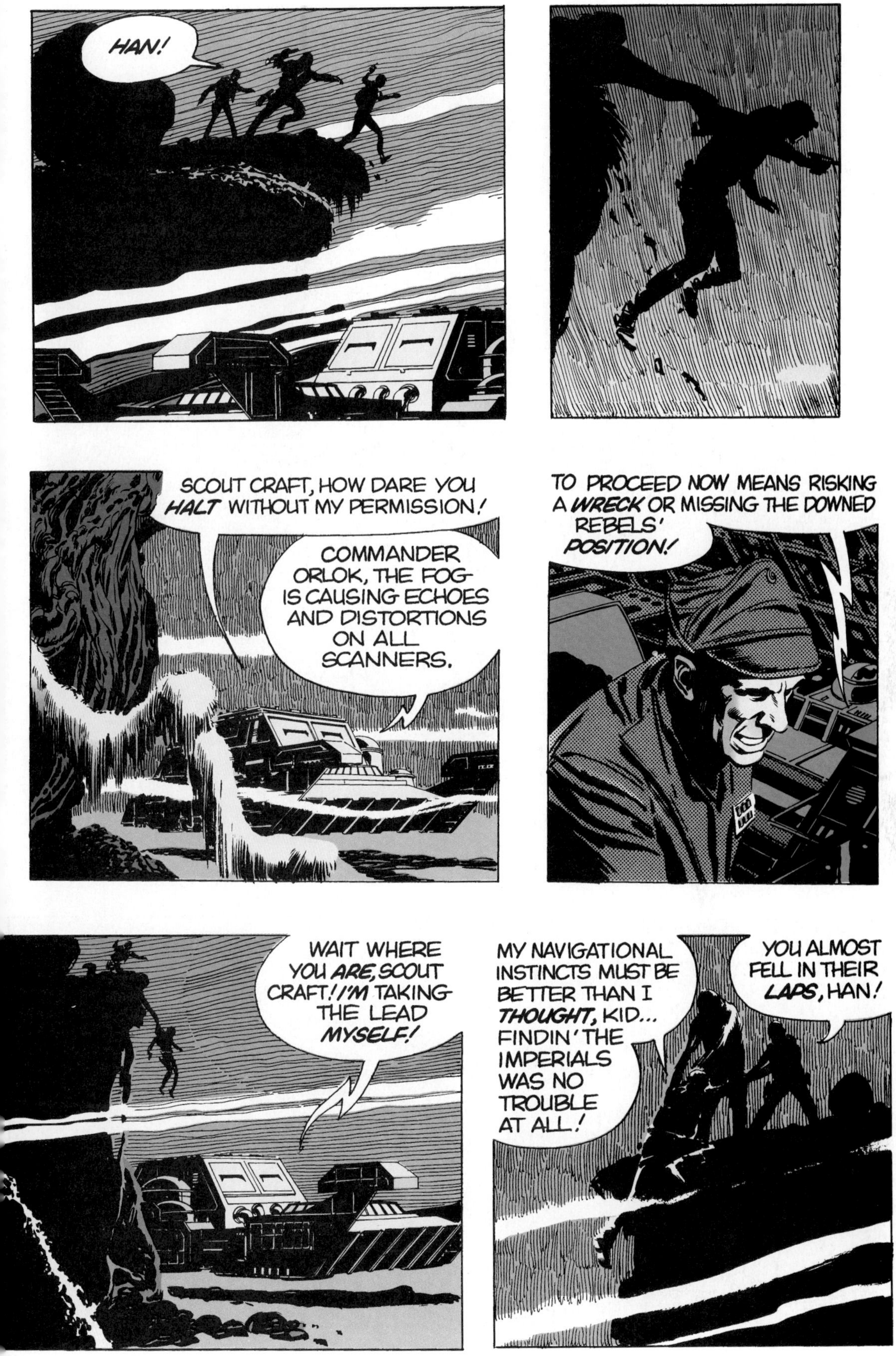
HAN!
SCOUT CRAFT, HOW DARE YOU HALT WITHOUT MY PERMISSION!
COMMANDER ORLOK, THE FOG IS CAUSING ECHOES AND DISTORTIONS ON ALL SCANNERS.
TO PROCEED NOW MEANS RISKING A WRECK OR MISSING THE DOWNED REBELS' POSITION!
WAIT WHERE YOU ARE, SCOUT CRAFT! I'M TAKING THE LEAD MYSELF!
MY NAVIGATIONAL INSTINCTS MUST BE BETTER THAN I THOUGHT, KID... FINDIN' THE IMPERIALS WAS NO TROUBLE AT ALL!
YOU ALMOST FELL IN THEIR LAPS, HAN!

YEAH,...MAYBE WE SHOULD DROP SOMETHIN' *ELSE* IN MY PLACE!

THEIR CRAFT'S *ARMORED!* EVEN THAT *BOULDER* WON'T DO MUCH DAMAGE!

TRUE! BUT IT MAY SORT'A ATTRACT THEIR *ATTENTION!*

CHEWIE, THIS IS *YOUR* KIND'A JOB!

Within the stalled Imperial scout craft... *SUDDEN SHOCK!*

SOMETHING'S *HIT* US! W-WHAT?!

A *BOULDER!* RAIN MUST HAVE LOOSENED IT!

WHAT *NEXT* FROM THIS MUDBALL WORLD?

THAT DEPENDS ON HOW *SENSIBLE* YOU HELMET-HEADS ARE ABOUT THROWING DOWN YOUR BLASTERS!

ONLY *TWO* REBELS! THEY CAN'T *OUTGUN* US ALL!

THIS IS JUST WHAT I WAS *AFRAID* OF, HAN!

RELAX, KID! WITH CHEWIE ON THE BLUFF *ABOVE* 'EM...

...WE *CAN* OUTGUN 'EM ALL!

BUT NOT WITHOUT MAKING *NOISE* ENOUGH TO ALERT THE *REST* OF THE IMPERIALS HEADED THIS WAY!

...THEY DIDN'T STAND A CHANCE!

NO, BUT THEY CAUSED US TO MAKE ENOUGH *NOISE* TO ALERT THEIR *MAIN PARTY!*

And... THE FOG IS *DISPERSING*, COMMANDER ORLOK! WE CAN RUSH TO *HELP* OUR ATTACKED SCOUT!

EXACTLY AS OUR ENEMY *EXPECTS!*

LISTEN, HAN... *SKIMMER ENGINES!* THE OTHER IMPERIALS ARE HEADED OUR WAY... *FAST!*

YEAH! AN' THE *WIND'S* COMIN' UP... BLOWIN' AWAY THIS *FOG* COVER!

JOIN CHEWIE UP ON THE *BLUFF*, KID! I'M GONNA TRY ARRANGIN' A *SURPRISE* FOR 'EM!

But as Luke starts *UP* the muddy slope...

CHEWBACCA! W-WHAT--?!

WAROWWWRRK!

Attempting to join Chewbacca *ATOP* the mud bluff...Luke finds himself *COLLIDING* with the Wookiee sliding *DOWN!*

CHEWIE! WHAT'S GOT INTO YOU?!

The *ANSWER* appears above...

IMPERIALS!

REBELS AREN'T THE *ONLY* ONES CAPABLE OF SURPRISES! MEN... *FIRE AT WILL!*

HAN! FIRE THAT THING UP AND GET US *OUT* OF HERE!

THE IMPERIALS USED THE SOUND OF THEIR APPROACHING *GROUND-SKIMMERS* TO COVER A LARGE PARTY OF 'EM SNEAKING *ABOVE* US ON *FOOT!*

MOVE! BEFORE WE'RE *TRAPPED* HERE!

I'M *DOIN'* IT, LUKE...BUT YOU SHOULD KNOW THERE ARE DEFINITE *DRAWBACKS!*

HAN, WE'VE GOT TWO *GROUND-SKIMMERS* APPROACHING AND STORMTROOPERS *ZEROING IN* FROM THE BLUFF! WHAT COULD BE *WORSE?!*

I FIGURED THE IMPERIALS WOULD BE TAKING THIS BABY *BACK*, LUKE! SO I CROSS-WIRED ITS POWER-CIRCUITRY TO *OVERLOAD...*

...ANY SECOND NOW, WE SHOULD *BLOW UP!*

THE REBEL AT THE GROUND-SKIMMER'S CONTROLS IS *AMAZING,* COMMANDER ORLOK! I'VE NEVER SEEN *ANYONE* DODGE FIRE LIKE THAT!

DON'T LET *UP...*

...THEY'RE HEADING STRAIGHT INTO RANGE OF *OUR* VEHICLES' GUNS!

HAN, WE CAN'T *MOVE!* AND WE CAN'T STAY PUT WITHOUT *BLOWING UP!* WHAT ARE WE GONNA *DO.?!*

KID... I'M OPEN TO *SUGGESTIONS!*

And back at the mud lake where the Mon Calamari are trying to raise the *MILLENNIUM FALCON...*

PRINCESS LEIA! *THERE...* IN THE *DISTANCE!*

SOMETHING *BIG* JUST EXPLODED!

WHAT DO ARTOO'S *SENSORS* SAY ABOUT IT?

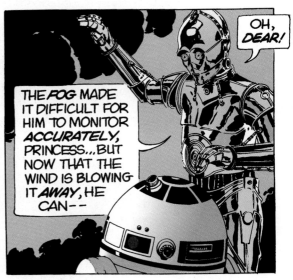

OH, *DEAR!*

THE *FOG* MADE IT DIFFICULT FOR HIM TO MONITOR *ACCURATELY,* PRINCESS... BUT NOW THAT THE WIND IS BLOWING IT *AWAY,* HE CAN--

ARTOO BELIEVES AN IMPERIAL *GROUND-SKIMMER* BLEW UP... AND HE FEARS MASTER LUKE, CAPTAIN SOLO, AND CHEWBACCA WERE *ABOARD* IT!

ARTOO MUST BE *MISTAKEN...*

HE *MUST* BE, YOUR HIGHNESS! THE ODDS ARE--

BRR-KLKKK TRRRWEEET *VOOOP!*

ARTOO-DETOO! SURELY, YOU'RE CAPABLE OF CALCULATING *BETTER ODDS* THAN THAT!

BAD NEWS OF SKYWALKER AND SOLO? I FEAR MY MON CALAMARI AND I HAVE NO GOOD WORDS TO *OFFSET* IT!

ADMIRAL ACKBAR! YOUR EFFORTS TO FREE THE *MILLENNIUM FALCON?*

FAILED, PRINCESS LEIA!

"THE SHIP IS *STILL* AT THE MUD LAKE BOTTOM...STILL IN THE COILS OF THE WORM-GIANTS THAT *DWELL* THERE..."

...THOUGH WE ATTACKED WITH *REPAIR TORCHES* ATTEMPTING TO DISLODGE THEM!

SOME DAYS THERE'S JUST NO *WINNING...* ESPECIALLY ON *THIS* PLANET!

HAN! LUKE!

CHEWBACCA, TOO, YOUR HIGHNESS! ALL *ALIVE!*

WE THOUGHT YOU WERE *KILLED* IN THE GROUND-SKIMMER EXPLOSION!

IT WAS *CLOSE!* WE MANAGED TO *DIVE OUT* JUST BEFORE IT *BLEW!*

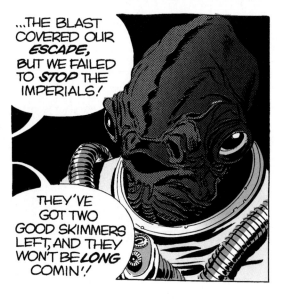

...THE BLAST COVERED OUR *ESCAPE,* BUT WE FAILED TO *STOP* THE IMPERIALS!

THEY'VE GOT TWO GOOD SKIMMERS LEFT, AND THEY WON'T BE *LONG* COMIN'!

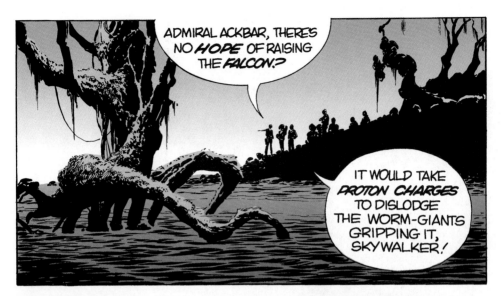

ADMIRAL ACKBAR, THERE'S NO *HOPE* OF RAISING THE *FALCON*?

IT WOULD TAKE *PROTON CHARGES* TO DISLODGE THE WORM-GIANTS GRIPPING IT, SKYWALKER!

EVEN IF WE *HAD* PROTON CHARGES... WE'D NEED 'EM AGAINST THOSE *IMPERIAL SKIMMERS* THAT'LL BE HUSTLIN' THIS WAY!

FROM ACROSS THE *MUD LAKE*? INTERESTING, CAPTAIN, *INTERESTING*?

WE USED ALL OUR *LUCK* HANDIN' THOSE IMPERIALS A *SMALL* LOSS, ADMIRAL ACKBAR! WITH THE *FALCON* STILL SUNK...

...AN' NOTHIN' BUT *HAND BLASTERS* TO USE AGAINST IMPERIAL SKIMMERS, I'M REAL RECEPTIVE TO *ANY* BRIGHT IDEAS!

WAIT, HAN...

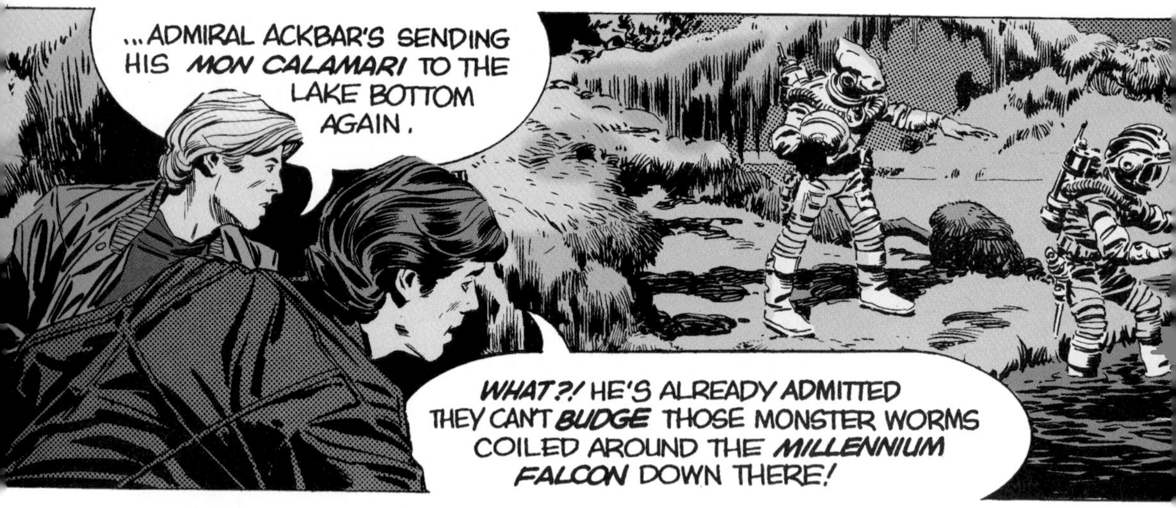
...ADMIRAL ACKBAR'S SENDING HIS *MON CALAMARI* TO THE LAKE BOTTOM AGAIN.
WHAT?! HE'S ALREADY ADMITTED THEY CAN'T *BUDGE* THOSE MONSTER WORMS COILED AROUND THE *MILLENNIUM FALCON* DOWN THERE!

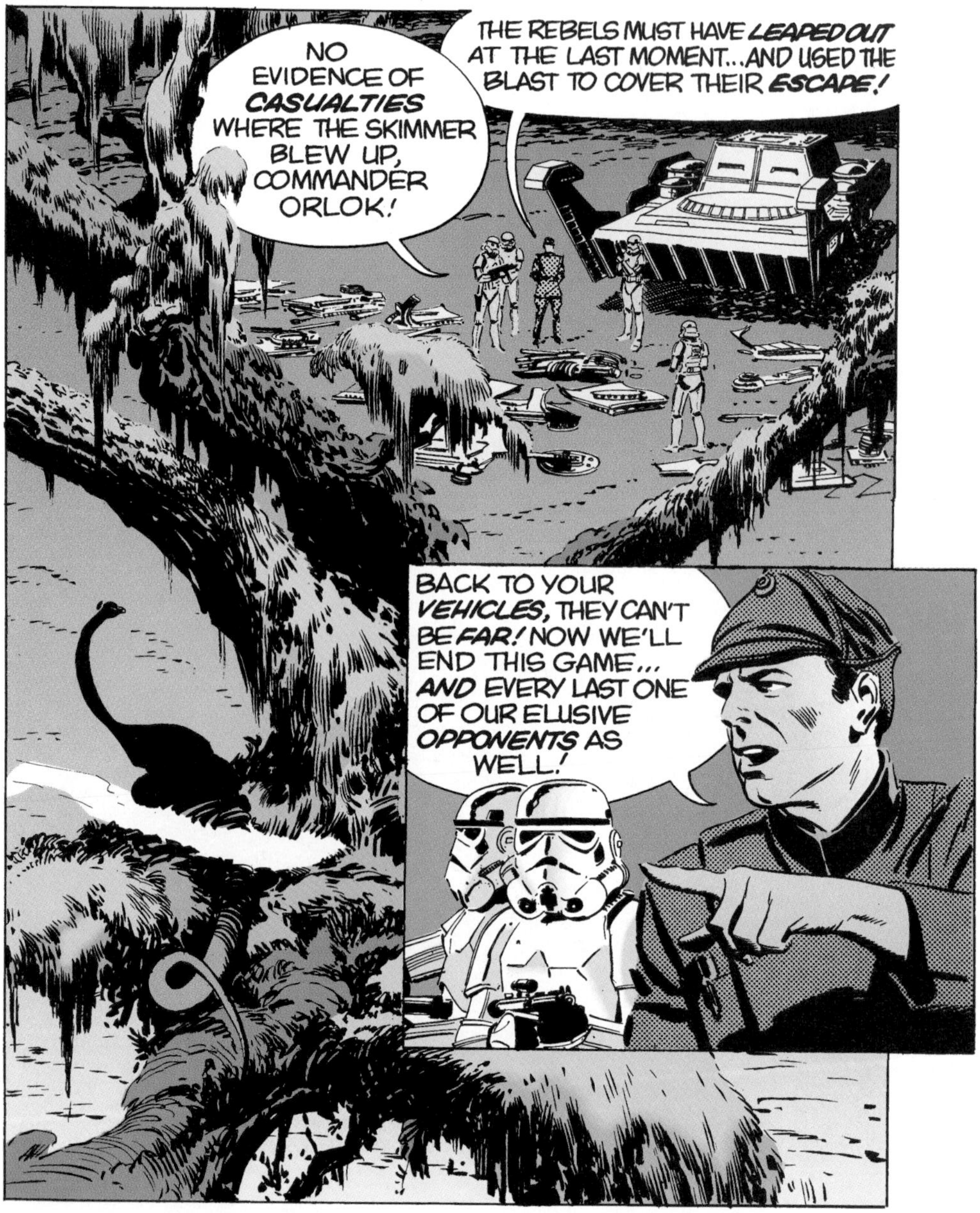
NO EVIDENCE OF *CASUALTIES* WHERE THE SKIMMER BLEW UP, COMMANDER ORLOK!
THE REBELS MUST HAVE *LEAPED OUT* AT THE LAST MOMENT...AND USED THE BLAST TO COVER THEIR *ESCAPE!*
BACK TO YOUR *VEHICLES*, THEY CAN'T BE *FAR!* NOW WE'LL END THIS GAME... *AND* EVERY LAST ONE OF OUR ELUSIVE *OPPONENTS* AS WELL!

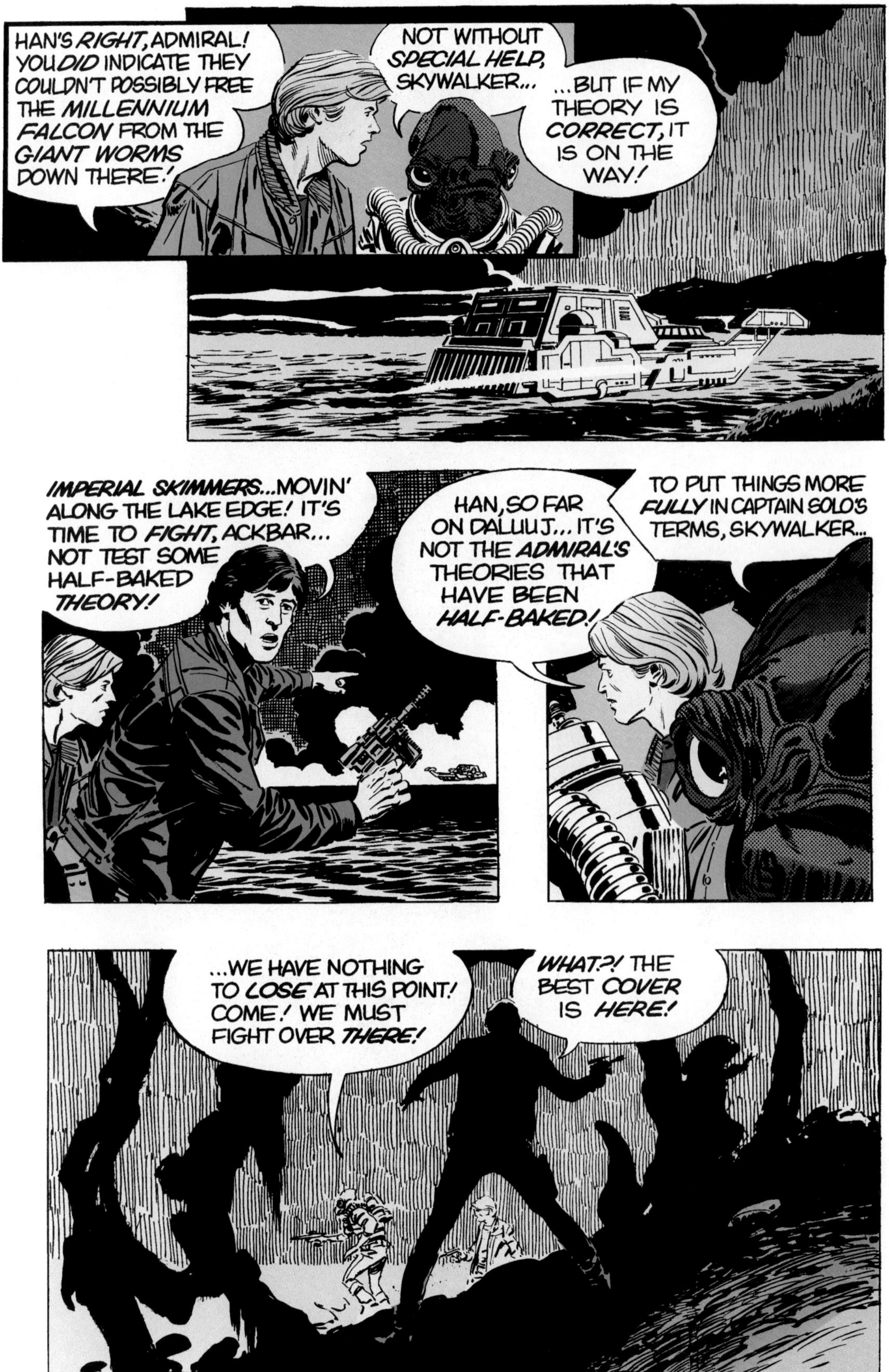
HAN'S RIGHT, ADMIRAL! YOU DID INDICATE THEY COULDN'T POSSIBLY FREE THE MILLENNIUM FALCON FROM THE GIANT WORMS DOWN THERE!
NOT WITHOUT SPECIAL HELP, SKYWALKER...
...BUT IF MY THEORY IS CORRECT, IT IS ON THE WAY!
IMPERIAL SKIMMERS...MOVIN' ALONG THE LAKE EDGE! IT'S TIME TO FIGHT, ACKBAR... NOT TEST SOME HALF-BAKED THEORY!
HAN, SO FAR ON DALUUJ... IT'S NOT THE ADMIRAL'S THEORIES THAT HAVE BEEN HALF-BAKED!
TO PUT THINGS MORE FULLY IN CAPTAIN SOLO'S TERMS, SKYWALKER...
...WE HAVE NOTHING TO LOSE AT THIS POINT! COME! WE MUST FIGHT OVER THERE!
WHAT?! THE BEST COVER IS HERE!

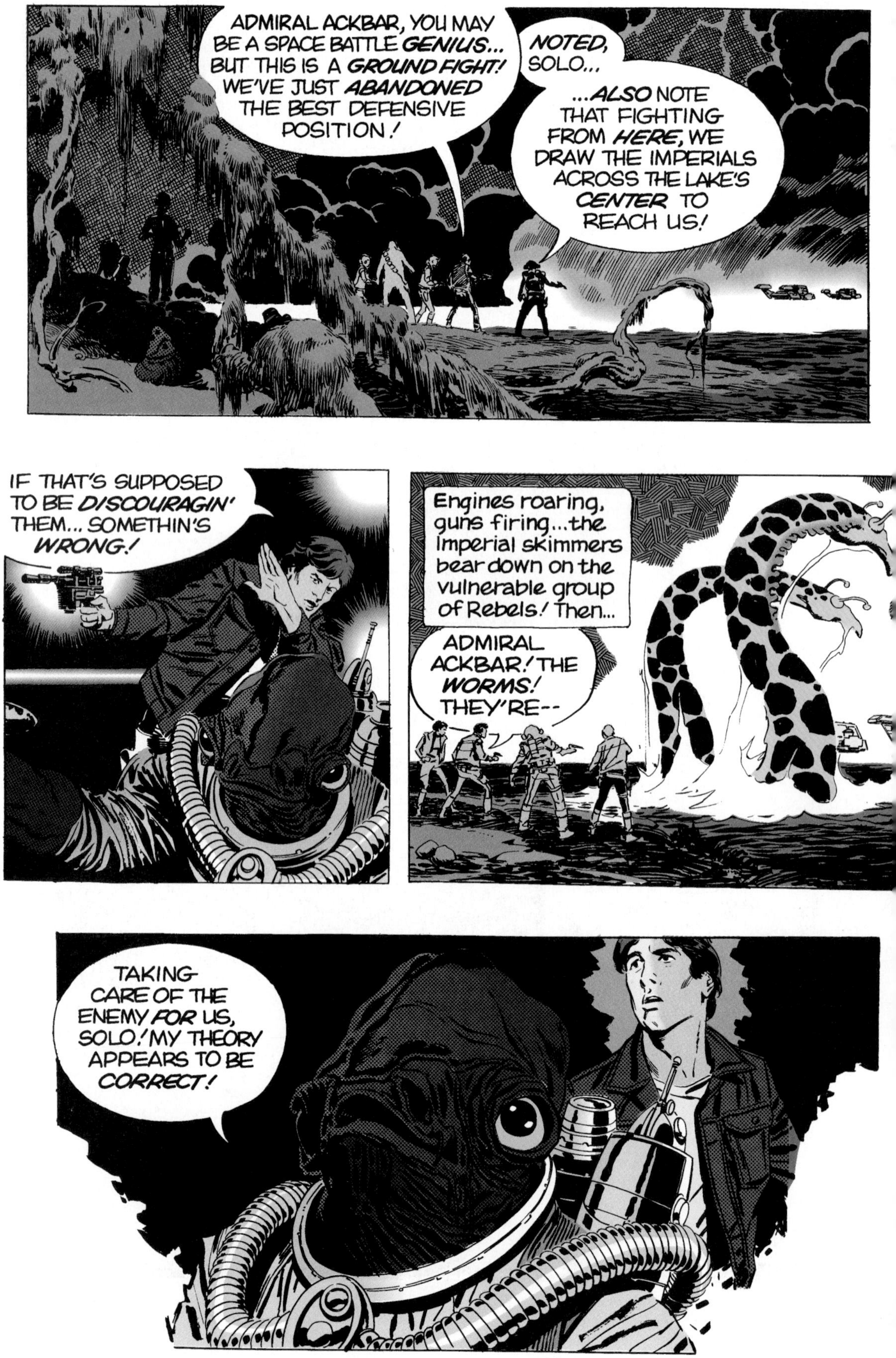
ADMIRAL ACKBAR, YOU MAY BE A SPACE BATTLE GENIUS... BUT THIS IS A GROUND FIGHT! WE'VE JUST ABANDONED THE BEST DEFENSIVE POSITION!
NOTED, SOLO...
...ALSO NOTE THAT FIGHTING FROM HERE, WE DRAW THE IMPERIALS ACROSS THE LAKE'S CENTER TO REACH US!
IF THAT'S SUPPOSED TO BE DISCOURAGIN' THEM... SOMETHIN'S WRONG!
Engines roaring, guns firing...the Imperial skimmers bear down on the vulnerable group of Rebels! Then...
ADMIRAL ACKBAR! THE WORMS! THEY'RE--
TAKING CARE OF THE ENEMY FOR US, SOLO! MY THEORY APPEARS TO BE CORRECT!

THE NOISE OR MOTION OF HEAVY MACHINES *IRRITATES* THEM INTO ATTACKING, ADMIRAL ACKBAR?

SOMETHING ATTRACTED THEM TO SOLO'S SHIP AS WELL AS THESE BATTLE VEHICLES, SKYWALKER...

...SO I SENT MY MON CALAMARI BELOW IN THE HOPE THAT *NEW AGITATION* WOULD MAKE THE CREATURES DO WHAT *WE* COULD NOT...

...RELEASE THE MILLENNIUM FALCON!

And blowing out mud and water, the smuggling craft lifts Rebels, droids, and Allies from Daluuj...

NO! NOW THAT WE'RE *FINISHED* WITH THIS MISERABLE PLANET...THE *SUN* COMES OUT!

Meanwhile, *OTHER* Rebel vessels face *NEW* challenges!

THAT'S OUR *TARGET?!* I-I NEVER DREAMED A SHIP COULD BE SO *HUGE*, CAPTAIN!

THEN WE SHOULDN'T HAVE ANY TROUBLE *HITTING* IT! COMMENCE *FIRING!*

LORD VADER! WE'RE UNDER *ATTACK* FROM A REBEL BATTLE CRUISER!

MAINTAIN OUR COURSE... LET THEM *COME!*

HOW MUCH *LONGER?* THOSE REBELS ARE *GOOD!* IF A SHIELD *WEAKENS...*

CONFIDENCE, ADMIRAL. YOU'RE NOT ABOARD ANY *ORDINARY* STAR DESTROYER.

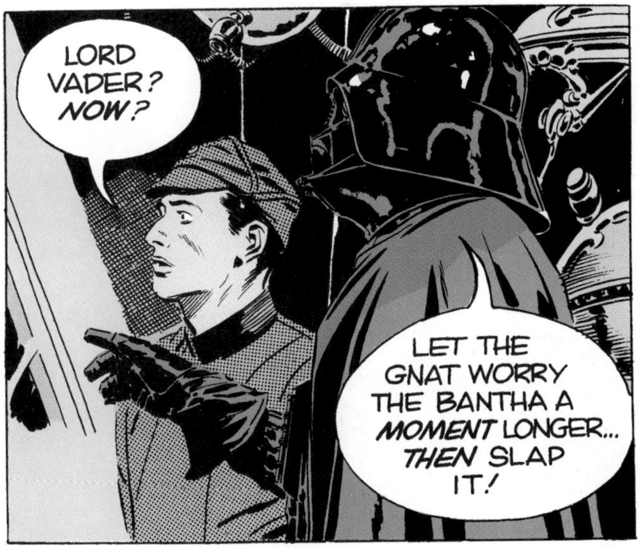
LORD VADER? *NOW?*
LET THE GNAT WORRY THE BANTHA A *MOMENT* LONGER... *THEN* SLAP IT!

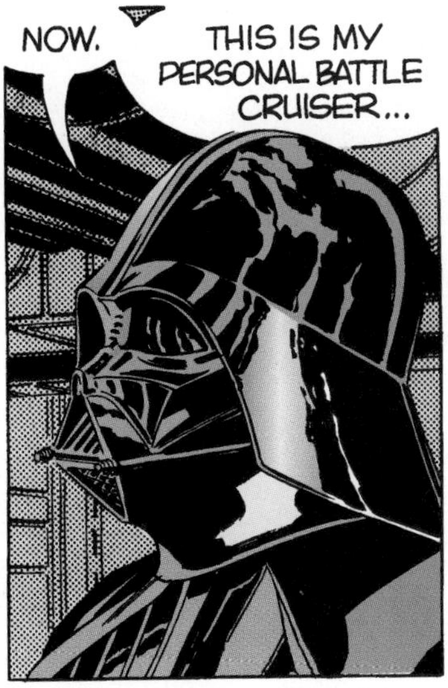
NOW.
THIS IS MY PERSONAL BATTLE CRUISER...

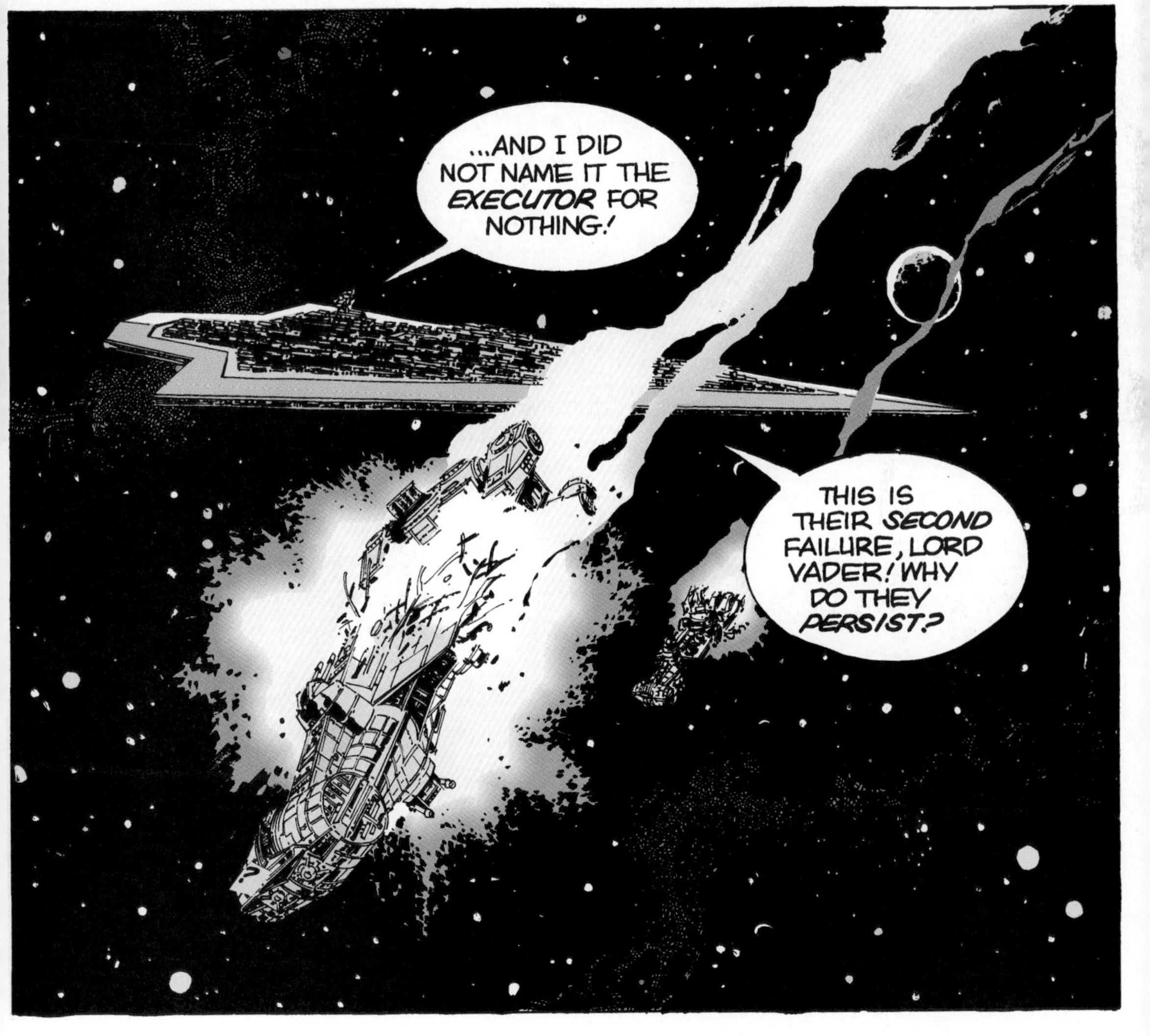
...AND I DID NOT NAME IT THE *EXECUTOR* FOR NOTHING!
THIS IS THEIR *SECOND* FAILURE, LORD VADER! WHY DO THEY *PERSIST?*

THE REBEL CRUISER IS *OBLITERATED*, LORD VADER! BUT... WHY DID YOU *DELAY* DOING IT?

SO THEY WOULD HAVE *TIME* TO REPORT TO THEIR HEADQUARTERS AND *CONFIRM* WHAT MUST ALREADY BE *SUSPECTED*, ADMIRAL...

...I AM GOING TO *DESTROY* THEIR BASE AT YAVIN AND *NOTHING* THEY HAVE CAN *STOP* ME!

PROCEED ON COURSE, ADMIRAL. DO NOT LET FURTHER ATTACKS *ALTER* OR *SLOW* OUR PROGRESS.

LORD VADER, THE REBELS WOULDN'T *DARE* STRIKE AGAIN!

THE ALLIANCE HAS NEVER *LACKED* FOR DARING, ADMIRAL. BUT AGAINST THE *EXECUTOR* THEY NEED FAR *MORE*...

...THEY NEED A *MIRACLE!*

The *EXECUTOR* continues on its relentless march through space...leaving in its wake the debris of the latest attempt by the Rebel Alliance to *STOP* it...

...debris about to be encountered by a *NEW* ship entering the system...

...the *MILLENNIUM FALCON.*

RUNNING THE IMPERIAL BLOCKADE IS *ALWAYS* TRICKY...BUT ONE MORE OF THESE HYPERSPACE HOPS OUGHT TO PUT US *HOME!*

HAN! THIS *DEBRIS*...

YEAH! WE JUST MISSED A *BATTLE,* LUKE! KEEP YOUR EYES PEELED...

...SO MUCH FLOATING JUNK CAN AFFECT OUR *SCOPES!*

As the young warrior scans the sector of space beyond his gun turret...

A *REBEL SCOUT SHIP* COMING FROM BEHIND THAT MOON!

For an instant, the Rebel scout craft streaks across Luke's field of vision from the *MILLENNIUM FALCON'S* gun turret. Then...

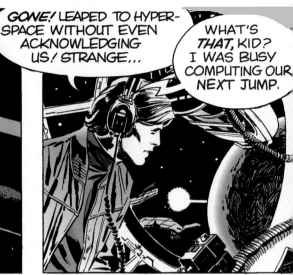

GONE! LEAPED TO HYPER-SPACE WITHOUT EVEN ACKNOWLEDGING US! STRANGE...

WHAT'S *THAT*, KID? I WAS BUSY COMPUTING OUR NEXT JUMP.

AND THE DROIDS ARE SHUT DOWN AND CHEWIE AN' LEIA ARE CATCHIN' SOME *SLEEP.* I GUESS IT'S NOT *IMPORTANT*, HAN...

Luke is *WRONG.*

THE FOURTH MOON OF YAVIN! After a circuitous series of hyperspace jumps to avoid the Imperial blockade...

...the *MILLENNIUM FALCON* returns to Rebel headquarters!

OUR MISSION WAS A *SUCCESS*, GENERAL DODONNA! WE HAD DIFFICULTIES...BUT OUR *MON CALAMARI* ALLIES AGREED TO *AID* IN OUR EVACUATION PLAN!

GENERAL DODONNA?

I-I'M SORRY, PRINCESS LEIA. *OTHER* NEWS I'VE RECEIVED IS,...NOT SO GOOD!

ALL ATTEMPTS TO SLOW THE APPROACH OF DARTH VADER'S BATTLE CRUISER HAVE *FAILED,* PRINCESS...

...INCLUDING AN ATTACK LED BY A SCOUT SHIP MY... *OWN SON* PILOTED!

SCOUT SHIP? LIKE I SAW ON OUR *WAY* HERE?!

Y-YOUR OWN *SON,* LOST ATTACKING DARTH VADER'S NEW SHIP? GENERAL DODONNA, I HAD *NO IDEA!* I'M SO--

YOU'VE SUFFERED *MORE,* PRINCESS. YOUR ENTIRE *PLANET* DESTROYED...

..I-I JUST NEED A BIT OF TIME...TO DEAL WITH THE *SHOCK...*

SHOULD I TELL HIM ABOUT THE *SCOUT SHIP* I GLIMPSED? WHAT IF IT *WASN'T* HIS SON'S?

GENERAL DODONNA!

LEIA, WE PASSED THROUGH A *BATTLE SITE* ON OUR WAY BACK HERE! I DON'T WANT TO RAISE THE GENERAL'S *HOPES,* BUT I THOUGHT I SAW--

COMMUNICATIONS REPORTS ONE OF OUR *SCOUT CRAFTS* COMING IN FOR A *CRASH LANDING,* SIR! IT APPEARS TO BE--

MY *SON'S* SHIP!

SOMEHOW HE'S *SURVIVED* THE BATTLE WITH DARTH VADER'S CRUISER!

I'M SURE I SAW THAT SAME SHIP *AFTER* THE BATTLE... ONLY IT WAS TOTALLY *UNDAMAGED!*

The laser-blasted Rebel scout craft skids to a halt...and a lone figure emerges!

VRAD!

MY SON, MY *SON!* WE THOUGHT DARTH VADER HAD DESTROYED *YOU* WITH THE OTHERS!

THAT MONSTER SHIP OF HIS *NEARLY* DID, FATHER...

...BY THE TIME I MADE *EMERGENCY REPAIRS* TO GET BACK IN THE BATTLE... IT WAS ALL OVER!

THAT DOESN'T FIT WITH WHAT I *SAW!*

THANK THE FORCE, YOU'RE ALIVE, *VRAD!*

I FEEL ASHAMED BEING THE *ONLY ONE* TO RETURN, LEIA...

...I WON'T *REST* UNTIL DARTH VADER *PAYS* FOR WHAT HIS CRUISER DID TO MY SQUADRON!

SON, WE'VE *SEEN* THE DAMAGE INFLICTED ON YOUR SCOUT SHIP...

...THERE'S *NO ONE* WHO COULD *BLAME* YOU FOR BEING UNABLE TO REJOIN THE BATTLE!

HAN, WHAT DO *YOU* THINK OF GENERAL DODONNA'S SON, VRAD?

IF HE COULD LAND THIS LASER-CHEWED WRECK, HE'S A *GOOD PILOT*, KID...

...AND FROM *HERE* IT LOOKS LIKE HE'S *ALSO* COMPETITION FOR THE PRINCESS THAT YOU AND I DON'T NEED!

MAYBE YOU'VE GOT EVIDENCE HE'S AN *IMPERIAL SPY?*

NO! I DON'T HAVE *EVIDENCE* OF ANYTHING...

HAN, WE PASSED THROUGH THE *AFTERMATH* OF THAT BATTLE WITH DARTH VADER'S CRUISER! I THINK I SAW VRAD DODONNA'S SHIP THEN...

...POPPING FROM *BEHIND* A LOCAL MOON! IT DIDN'T HAVE *ANY* OF THESE DAMAGES!

KID, THAT *SOUNDS* LIKE YOU'RE HINTIN' A *GENERAL'S* SON AND REBEL *HERO*...

...DUCKED THE *FIGHT* AND INFLICTED THE DAMAGE HIMSELF TO *COVER UP!*

I *KNOW* WHAT I SAW, HAN...

...VRAD'S SHIP FLEEING FROM COVER, TOTALLY UNHARMED... *AFTER* THE COMBAT WHERE HE *SUPPOSEDLY* SUSTAINED TOO MUCH DAMAGE TO CONTINUE!

WE CAN'T LET THAT *PASS!*

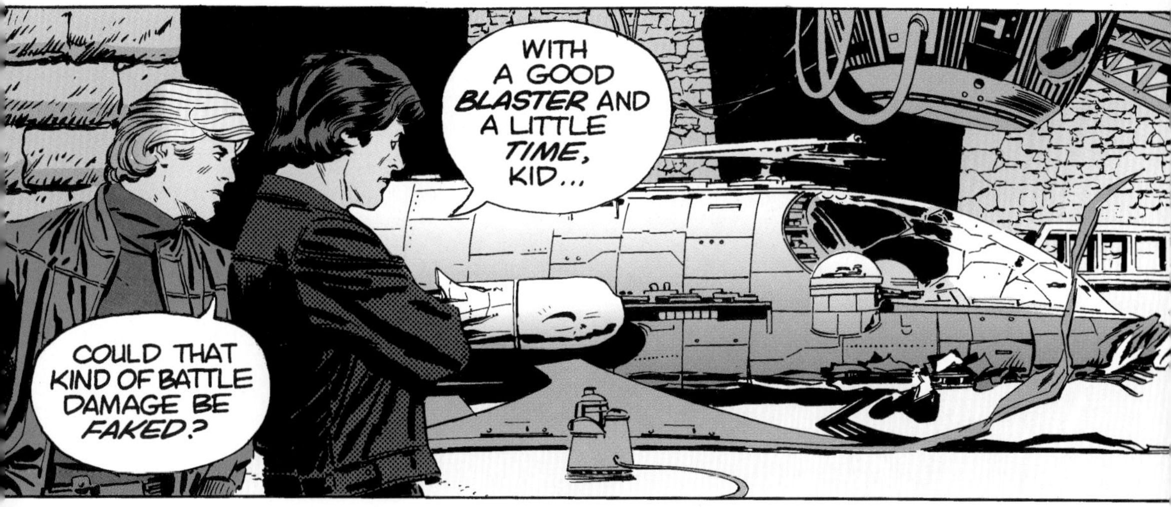
COULD THAT KIND OF BATTLE DAMAGE BE FAKED?
WITH A GOOD BLASTER AND A LITTLE TIME, KID...

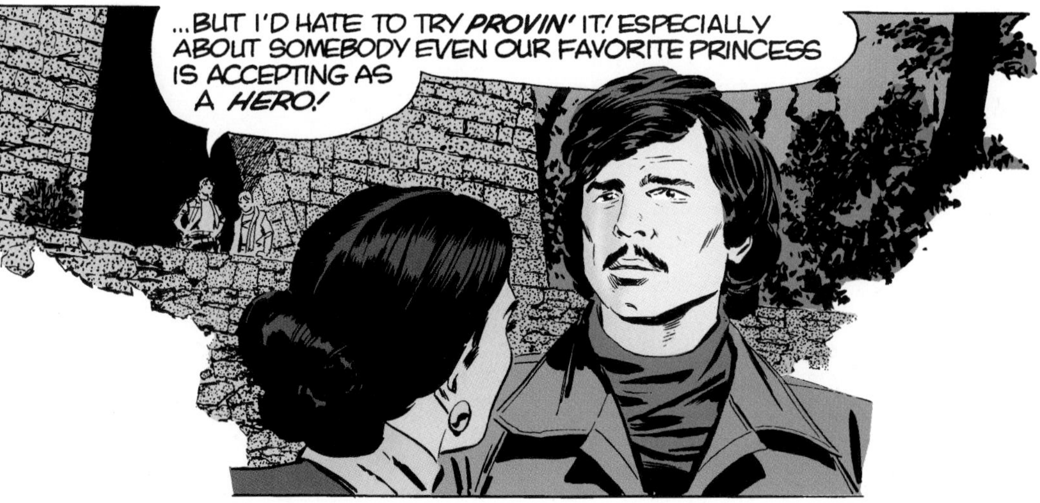
...BUT I'D HATE TO TRY PROVIN' IT! ESPECIALLY ABOUT SOMEBODY EVEN OUR FAVORITE PRINCESS IS ACCEPTING AS A HERO!

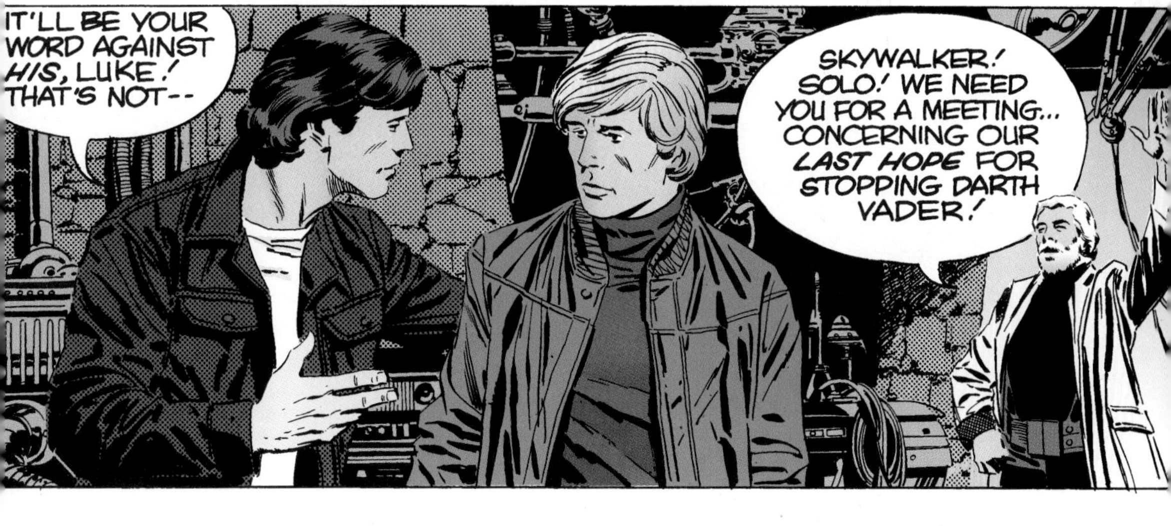
IT'LL BE YOUR WORD AGAINST HIS, LUKE! THAT'S NOT--
SKYWALKER! SOLO! WE NEED YOU FOR A MEETING... CONCERNING OUR LAST HOPE FOR STOPPING DARTH VADER!

YOU *STILL* HOPE TO STOP DARTH VADER'S GIANT CRUISER GENERAL?

FROM WHAT I'VE HEARD... IT CAN'T BE DONE!

SOLO, HAVE YOU, OF ALL PEOPLE, FORGOTTEN THE *POWER GEM?*

THE *POWER GEM?* WHAT *IS* IT, GENERAL DODONNA?!

SOLO HERE WENT THROUGH A GREAT DEAL TO *FIND* THIS FOR US, SKYWALKER...

CHEWIE AND I DID IT WHILE YOU WERE OFF ON ANOTHER *MISSION,* KID,...JUST TO KEEP FROM GETTING *RUSTY.*

GENERAL DODONNA, IF THIS IS YOUR *LAST HOPE* FOR STOPPING DARTH VADER...THE REBEL ALLIANCE IS IN *BIG TROUBLE!*

OUR SCIENTISTS TELL ME THE *POWER GEM* IS ACTUALLY SOME RARE METEORITE PARTICLE, SOLO... IT RADIATES A STRANGE *AURA.*

SPACE PIRATES ONCE DISCOVERED THE *SAME THING,* GENERAL...

"...INCLUDING THE FACT THAT THAT AURA COULD *DISRUPT* ANY SHIP'S *ENERGY SHIELD!*"

"BUT THAT WAS A LONG *TIME* AGO...*TOO LONG!*"

THERE'S A BIG *CATCH*, LUKE! IT'S THE *LAST* OF ITS KIND...AN' IT'S *LOSIN'* ITS POWER!

USIN' IT AGAINST VADER'S CRUISER IS *RISKY* AT BEST...AN' *SHEER SUICIDE* IF THE GEM POOPS OUT!

HAN, IF THIS *POWER GEM* CAN DISRUPT *ANY* SHIP'S ENERGY SHIELD...IT'S JUST WHAT'S NEEDED AGAINST *DARTH VADER'S* CRUISER!

WE *KNOW* WHAT A LARGE RISK IT IS THAT THE *POWER GEM* MAY FAIL AGAINST VADER'S *SHIELD SYSTEM*, SOLO...

THEN WHAT ARE WE *DOIN'* HERE, GENERAL DODONNA?

WHY...DECIDING WHICH OF THE THREE BEST *PILOTS* ON THE BASE WILL *DO* THE JOB! YOU, SKYWALKER... OR MY SON, *VRAD!*

"A SMALL *ATTACK SHIP* CARRYING THE GEM...

"...COULD DO WHAT OTHERWISE MIGHT REQUIRE A *FLEET...*

"...PENETRATE THE SHIELDS OF DARTH VADER'S CRUISER AND INFLICT DAMAGE ENOUGH TO *STOP* IT!"

WHAT YOU'VE GOT HERE IS A KIND OF *SUICIDE MISSION* GENERAL DODONNA! HOW DO YOU *DECIDE* WHO GETS TO HANDLE IT?

I WAS *HOPING* FOR *VOLUNTEERS,* CAPTAIN SOLO.

HOWEVER, SINCE THE GEM IS *LOSING* ITS POWER, THE RISKS ARE--

THERE'S NO NEED TO GO OVER THIS *AGAIN,* FATHER... *I* VOLUNTEER!

NO!

YOU HAVE SOME *OBJECTION* TO MY SON HANDLING THIS MISSION, SKYWALKER?

I...I'M A BETTER *PILOT*, GENERAL! *I* SHOULD GO INSTEAD!

Unable to prove his *REAL* objections to General Dodonna's son...Luke argues to take his place!

HAVE YOU FORGOTTEN THE *DEATH STAR*, SIR? THAT WAS A *MUCH* WORSE SITUATION.

SKYWALKER, I *KNOW* YOU'RE THE HERO OF THE DEATH STAR...BUT THIS WILL BE A *SHIP*-AGAINST-*SHIP* ENCOUNTER!

"CHECK THE *COMPUTER!* WHEN IT COMES TO *THAT* TYPE OF ACTION, YOU'LL FIND *ONE NAME* WAY AHEAD ON *EXPERIENCE*...

"...MINE: *VRAD DODONNA!*"

GENERAL DODONNA, THIS SITUATION IS GONNA *FORCE* ME TO BRING UP SOMETHING I DIDN'T WANT TO ABOUT YOUR *SON* AND--

I ALREADY *KNOW* SKYWALKER...

...YOU FEEL IF I PICK HIM OVER *YOU* FOR THIS MISSION, I'M PLAYING *FAVORITES!* PERFECTLY UNDERSTANDABLE. AND I HAVE A *SOLUTION!*

A MISSION SO IMPORTANT TO OUR SUCCESSFUL EVACUATION OF THIS BASE *SHOULDN'T* BE ENTRUSTED TO ONE MAN. YOU'LL ACCOMPANY MY SON, SKYWALKER... AS *BACK-UP PILOT!*

TERRIFIC, KID... INSTEAD OF *STOPPING* VRAD DODONNA...

...YOU'VE TALKED YOURSELF INTO BEING HIS *PARTNER* ON A *SUICIDE MISSION!*

THIS MAY BE *BEST*, HAN, I DON'T HAVE TO *HURT* GENERAL DODONNA BY DENOUNCING HIS SON...

...AND I'LL BE ALONG TO SEE VRAD DOESN'T *RUN OUT* LIKE BEFORE!

EVEN IF IT *KILLS* YOU?

As final preparations for the strike against Darth Vader are made...

SKYWALKER, IF SOMETHING ABOUT ME *BOTHERS* YOU...LET'S SETTLE IT *NOW!*

I HOPE I'M *WRONG* ABOUT WHAT'S BOTHERING ME, VRAD, BECAUSE I ADMIRE YOUR *FATHER*...

...BUT IF I'M *RIGHT,* AT LEAST I'LL BE ALONG TO SEE WHAT HAPPENED ON YOUR *LAST* MISSION DOESN'T HAPPEN ON *THIS* ONE!

WHAT DO YOU *THINK* HAPPENED ON MY LAST MISSION, SKYWALKER?

FOR SOME REASON, MAYBE EVEN A *GOOD* ONE...

...YOU *RAN OUT* ON THE BATTLE WITH DARTH VADER'S CRUISER AND *FAKED* DAMAGE TO YOUR SHIP TO COVER IT UP!

YOU SELF-RIGHTEOUS LITTLE TWERP, I OUGHT TO--

ARE YOU AND LUKE HAVING A *DISAGREEMENT,* VRAD? THIS MISSION IS TOO *IMPORTANT* TO ALLOW--

JUST DISCUSSING *ATTACK TECHNIQUES,* PRINCESS...

...*RIGHT*, SKYWALKER?

AND STRAIGHTENING OUT SOME DETAILS TO MAKE *CERTAIN* THIS MISSION WORKS AS IT'S *SUPPOSED* TO!

LET'S SETTLE THIS WHERE WE WON'T BE *INTERRUPTED*, HERO!

Luke and Vrad head for the woods...

THIS IS GOOD ENOUGH, SKYWALKER! GET READY TO *FIGHT!*

IF I'M *WRONG* ABOUT YOU, VRAD...THIS *ISN'T* THE WAY TO SETTLE IT!

MAYBE *NOT*, SKYWALKER...

...BUT WHEN IT'S *OVER*, YOU WON'T BE IN ANY SHAPE TO GO ON THE *MISSION* WITH ME!

WHERE ARE VRAD AND LUKE, GENERAL DODONNA? THE *POWER GEM* IS BEING MOUNTED ON THEIR CRAFT.

GOING OVER FINAL DETAILS OF THEIR *MISSION*, I'D ASSUME, PRINCESS.

The adventure continues
in CLASSIC STAR WARS

CLASSIC STAR WARS COVER GALLERY

Cover for issue 8 by Mark Schultz

"I remember seeing a huge ad in the *New York Times* for the first *Star Wars* movie and feeling skeptical," says Mark Schultz, "but after months of positive reviews, I got time off from my night job and stood in line — only to be turned away!" He did eventually see it . . . five months later.

Schultz's earliest *Star Wars* work was a trading card for Topps' first *Star Wars Galaxy* card set. The card depicts Luke, wearing his macrobinoculars, on Tatooine, with the bones of a creature at his feet.

For this cover, Schultz says he tried unsuccessfully to draw the demonsquid just like Al Williamson's and finally used an octopus as reference. The finished art, which obscures part of the *Star Wars* logo, was specially approved, with a warning that future cover art would be designed around the logo. "I like to think that I had a part in defining the limits of what Lucasfilm approves," says Schultz with a chuckle.

Cover for issue 9 by Al Williamson

"Before I even had a chance to see the first movie, people were calling me, saying, 'You've got to see this film! The guy who did it is a huge fan of yours; it has your name all over it.'" Did Al Williamson finally see it? "Oh, God, yes. And I loved it! Still do . . . Took the kids to see it at least eight times."

Williamson's first *Star Wars* gig was a sample daily newspaper strip for George Lucas. Lucasfilm asked if Al had any suggestions for a writer, and that's when he put in a plug for Archie Goodwin. The rest is history.

Cover for issue 10 by Al Williamson

"I think it's great to have different artists doing the covers. I've worked with each of these guys. They're all good friends of mine. Darned good artists too!" says Al Williamson when asked what he thinks about some of the *Classic Star Wars* covers being done by other artists.

"I didn't realize the impact *Star Wars* would have on me until several years later when I picked up one of *The Empire Strikes Back* comic books done by Al Williamson, which I ogled, thinking, if the movie is even half this good . . . " says Allen Nunis.

Nunis' first *Star Wars* gig was illustration work for West End Games' *Star Wars* role-playing game books. It was this work that eventually put him in touch with Al Williamson.

"It's important for a cover to illustrate a scene from the book," says Nunis, "but this cover gave too much away, so we had to save it for the issue after the one with this particular scene between Vader and Kenobi."

"I was old enough to actually drive to see the first *Star Wars* movie. But I had no idea how rich it was going to be," says Brett Blevins. "The John Williams score impressed me. And I was tickled that the main characters were so noble because" he says, "I'm a bit of an optimist."

Blevins' first *Star Wars* work was a Marvel comic-book cover, featuring Luke and a big, scary droid with a steel jaw and a mechanical eye.

On this cover: "The duel was the thing to do!"

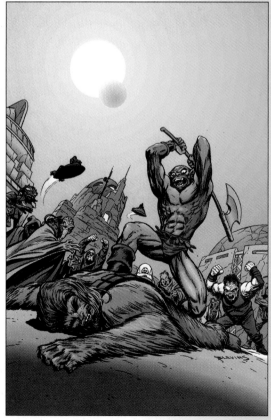

"I loved the concept of the Force," says Yeates who remembers seeing the first *Star Wars* movie in a New York theater while seated near a group of extremely enthusiastic kids who prefaced each scene with, "Check this part out!" and "This part's baaaaad!"

Yeates' first *Star Wars* work was the teeny bit of assistance on *The Empire Strikes Back* that Al Williamson would let him do while he was hanging out at Williamson's studio. "Something that actually has my 'stamp' on it though, is a dream sequence in the *Star Wars* comic *The Crimson Forever*.

Yeates remembers having to redo this particular cover: "My original renderings of the worm creatures weren't approved, so I had to redesign them."

"There's just something magical about *Star Wars . . .*"

—Al Williamson